Last Words?

A COLLECTION OF THE BEST

Phillip Adams

Foreword by Laura Tingle

WP

WP

Published by Wilkinson Publishing Pty Ltd
ACN 006 042 173
PO Box 24135, Melbourne, VIC 3001, Australia
Ph: +61 3 9654 5446
enquiries@wilkinsonpublishing.com.au
www.wilkinsonpublishing.com.au

WilkinsonPublishing
wilkinsonpublishinghouse

Title: Last Words? A collection of the best.
ISBN: 9781923259010: Printed – Paperback

Design by Michael Bannenberg.

Printed and bound in Australia by Ligare.

CONTENTS

Foreword vii
Introduction ix

2021

Scouts 1
Disneyland 3
Masks 5
Olden Days 7
Nostalgia Sequel 9
Ghost Story 13
Unlove Letters 15
Public Libraries 17
Philip 19
Birthdays 21
Frontline 23
Goya 25
In the Beginning 27
First Memories 29
Sherlock Jones 35
Art Critics 37
Signatures 39
Thought versus Sport 41
Detectives 43
Dogs in Heaven 45
Lan Choo Coupons 47
Body Parts 49
Catching Covid 51
Audio Books 53
NDE 55
Arthur Hodges 57

2022

Memory 60
Republic 62
Nuddy Pole 64

Risk Assessment 66
Votes for Trees 68
Bill Smith 70
Hawke 72
Elephant Man 74
Bottom's Up 76
Cooking 78
Snakes Alive 80
Election Day 82
Laughter 84
Failed State 86
John Clarke 88
Oz Movies 90
Top Gun 92
Cinema Violence 94
Mikhail 96
Roo the Day 98
Petty 100
Happy 102
Vroom Vroom 104
Dictionary 106
The Crown 108
In Black and White 110

2023

Slang 113
Sunburnt 115
Favourite Films 117
Pyramid Scheme 119
The Tree 121
Reading 123
Aphorisms 125
Happiness 127
Paper Papers 129
Isms 131
Petting 134
Ignorant 136
Tortoise 138
Qantas 140

Honest John 142
In a Jam 144
Super 146
My Way 148
The Gunited States 150
Scouts 152
Malcolm X 154
The A Bomb 156
Tree Hugging 158
Parky 160
Julian 162
Horrorscope 164
Australia Rhymes with Failure 166
Dig Deep 168

2024

Times 172
The Interview 174
Who Killed Julius Ceasar? 176
Roo 179
Exit Stage Left 181
Friends 183
End Times 185
Crash 187
Tony 189
Happy Birthday? 191
Salesman 193
Billions 195
Silence 197
Country Life 199
News 201
Ambassador Adams 203
Public Speaking 205
Towers 207
Cops 209
Pud 211

Foreword

Phillip Adams has been having much too much fun in his life. Really.

He and I spoke on the radio every Monday night for close to twenty years, but I always had this sneaking suspicion it was the least fun bit of his week.

Sometimes Phil's producers would try to jazz it up by adding other people to the conversation. But it never seemed to quite work. So he was stuck with me for the duration.

He was always trying to lead me astray into controversial opinions and territory on which I wouldn't, or couldn't, express an opinion.

But it all ultimately related to Australian politics, a subject which has sadly felt like it has shrunk a bit during those decades. Not a lot of big ideas.; a sense of a diminishing size of personalities.

We ploughed on nonetheless, having fun despite the topic, and the odd argument. As he farewelled me each Monday, he would preview the rich diversity of people he was going to speak to, about a richly diverse series of topics, leaving me nodding off to sleep feeling a little dull by comparison.

And then he would turn his attention to his column for *The Australian*: where the fun really seemed to start.

How do I get a job, or a brain, where I can cover subjects as broad as suicide, wine snobs, Tarzan, Beethoven, whether should you delete dead people's numbers from your phone, and geopolitics?

It turns out this is a job for a one-off talent: my dear friend Phillip. And here is the latest collection of his musings to celebrate. Where on earth will he go next?

Laura Tingle

Introduction

Last Words? Though recently retired from my role as the ABC's most ancient broadcaster I can still claim the title of Australia's most ancient columnist. My first efforts appeared in *The Guardian* when I was 16 – the same year ASIO opened their file on me. Comrade Adams – the youngest person to have attracted their anti-subversive attentions. (*The Guardian*? Let us absolve from ideological guilt the vaguely leftist newspaper born in Manchester. I speak of – and wrote for – the full-blown commo paper published in a back alley in Melbourne).

In the sixty years since my battered by-line has appeared beneath many an auspicious and in some case extinct masthead – *The Bulletin, Nation, The National Times, Nation Review, Australian Business, The Sydney Morning Herald, The Courier Mail, The Adelaide Advertiser, The Launceston Examiner* and, on and off for 60 years, in *The Australian*, where my politics are contrapuntal to the editorial line. Plus, I've quilled some prose for *The Times* in London and the 'Grey Lady' – aka *The New York Times.*

Such efforts are usually and justifiably evanescent. Read today, or perhaps glanced at, and gone tomorrow, in the proud tradition of 'the fish-wrap'. But from time to time over the decades I put together a few in a book like this – poshed up with an intro from such goods and greats as Gough Whitlam, Alan Marshall, Michael Kirby, Richard Flanagan and, in this case, by beloved friend and colleague Laura. Sadly, this will probably be my final 'mingle with Tingle' – unless she taps out an obit.

Hence the poignant question of the title: 'Last Words?'

Despite accepting an advance from Penguin decades ago – about the same time as Wes Walters painted the portrait of the youthful me that provides our cover (winner of the Archibald in, FFS, 1979) I have never and will never write an autobiography. Let 70 years of newspaper and magazine columns serve as a censored substitute.

The first such collection got its title from a piece of hate mail – a Letter to the Editor at *The Age* – wherein an angry lady complained of 'the unwholesome waffle of the unspeakable Adams'.

Her last three words worked well on the cover. The Unspeakable Adams. Here, a lifetime later, is more unwholesome waffle.

Thanks for reading it.

2021

Scouts

While chatting to Peter Fitzsimons about his book *Breaker Morant* the name of Baden-Powell came up. 'The Hero of Mafeking' who, after leading British soldiers against unruly Zulus and Boers returned home to establish his 'broomstick warriors', to whom, decades later, I'd belong. Until, like the Breaker, I'd be court-martialled and drummed from the regiment.

While Morant was as guilty as hell my trial was a travesty. Though spared the firing squad, and though now 81, I was planning to sue the Scouts for dosh and reputational damage. For embarrassing reasons they dropped 'Boy' from 'Boy Scouts' years ago. But my timing's out. I now discover Baden-Powell is broke.

Well, at least in the US where they've declared bankruptcy – because they're facing claims from almost 90,000 Scouts reporting sexual molestation. Those figures make the Scouts second only to the Roman Catholic Church when it comes to paedophilia.

Notwithstanding the Scouts' legal manoeuvrings, I demand justice in 2021. Let me tell you what happened to young Phillip.

After being a member of the prepubescent cubs in East Kew my family decamped to East Melbourne where I was promoted to a Boy Scout troop that met in the basement of a massive bluestone Anglican Church. Here we earned badges for tying knots – something very difficult for a left-hander. We also went on camping trips with weren't camp in the least. No Scoutmasters misbehaved. But we Scouts did, in all sorts of ways. Which takes me back to the bluestone basement.

Officialdom, i.e the Scoutmaster, hadn't arrived so my fellow Scouts were sharing a packet of Turf, then the cheapest cigarette brand. Ten of us, one each. Puffing away and coughing like mad. When we heard the Scoutmaster on the stairs. Being prepared – Baden-Powell's instruction to Scouts the world over – I grabbed our ciggies and shoved them in the drawer of his desk. And we lined up, all innocence, for 'inspection'. This involved standing at attention whilst the superior officer checked our uniforms and woggles, whatever they were.

Then the Scoutmaster stiffened, if you'll forgive the expression, and sniffed the air. As well he might, given it stank of smoke. The smoke coming out of his drawer. The smoke caused by the burning smokes I'd shoved into it. And suddenly the desk was ablaze. With smoke billowing the Anglican Reverent, having called the fire brigade, thundered into the basement and demanded the name of the arsonist.

All the Scouts – and the Scoutmaster – pointed at Adams. I was forced then and there to hand over my woggle and shown the door as the fire brigade arrived. One of their easier jobs. The blaze was extinguished in a few seconds. The only damage was the desk and my previously pristine reputation.

Out of the Scouts at 13 I'd join the Communist Party at 15 – to become the only child with an ASIO file, though I wouldn't get to see it for another 40 years. Naturally I expected ASIO to have all the dirt, my full criminal record with my attempt to incinerate an Anglican church linked to my intention to raze Australian democracy. But that section, like much in my ASIO file, seems heavily redacted.

Back to my trial. Note that I had no legal representation. I couldn't call character witnesses. Not even mum knew I was on charges. Given the Scouts are bust I'll not demand a big payout. It's not about money. All I want is an apology and the return of my woggle. OK, OK, I confess. Like Breaker Morant I was as guilty as hell. But aren't we all?

Disneyland

Today's theme? Theme parks. In popular culture the most famous is Disneyland but they have, of course, a more venerable history. Long before the Walt Dynasty founded their first in Anaheim the Egyptian dynasties built whoppers from Aswan to Alexandria, via Karnak and the Great Pyramids.

And what else is London than a theme park? For the British Monarchy, from Buckingham and Windsor Palaces to the Tower of London. The Vatican? A theme park for Roman Catholicism's sins of the fathers. Wall Street? A theme park for the sins of capitalism. Melbourne's Shrine of Remembrance? A theme park for the mythologizing of the military.

Welcome first to Disneyland, aka the Magic Kingdom, ruled over by a royal mouse and dukedoms of both ducks (Donald etc) of dogs (Goofy and Pluto}. Plus Snow White and her seven diminutive disciples and a collection of audio-animatronic robots vaguely resembling dead and dying Presidents. More of them later.

But Walt's enterprise is dwarfed by a mightier kingdom than his Magic Kingdom – the biggest theme park of them all. Washington DC. Embodying 'manifest destiny' and the US' version/vision/parody of democracy. The scale is meant to intimidate, its architecture borrowing heavily from Ancient Rome, Greece and Egypt. Giant domes. Awesome temples. Mighty obelisks. But like Disneyland it turns out to be as fragile as a Hollywood set, ready to be destroyed by a few thousand over-acting extras.

Enter stage right – far right – Donald J. Trump. I haven't been to a Disneyland for decades and there are branches in Florida, Japan, Europe and for all I know on the Gold Coast. So I don't know if there are high-tech Tussaud's boasting audio-animatronic Donalds on display (Is this Donald perhaps a relative of Disneys?) or whether he's been removed from display as he was from Twitter.

Recently, as you may have heard, the actual Donald J Trump called upon his followers to destroy the DC theme park. If he couldn't have it then nobody could. Followers dressed in silly suits (rather like the poor sweating staff of Disneyland dressed up as Goofy) charged the Capitol to wreak havoc, hang the Veep and kill the elected reps and staff.

Disneyland(s) offer a choice of wild rides, but none as wilder than those proposed by DJT. Come and destroy not the faux-imperial buildings but the very idea they're meant to inspire. As Louis XV said 'après moi le deluge'. Forget such minor events as the Storming of the Bastille or the Bolshevik's Storming of the Winter Palace. From the President who gave us Stormy Daniels' here's an order to storm the citadel of the American Dream. I had a flashback to the Fall of Saigon, fully expecting to see desperate survivors fighting for that last helicopter ride from the roof. With Trump escaping in his last helicopter ride from the White House lawn, giving Nixon's 'V for victory' finger signs.

Totally appropriate to a President fleeing a crime scene – with the 400,000 Corona deaths exceeding the US death toll in Vietnam. Ideas blur and overlap – Agent Orange and the Orange president.

Donald, we hardly knew you. And we will miss you and your delightful family dreadfully. Please come back soon. Please run again in 2024. Meantime we'll make do with the audio-animatronic doppelganger.

Well, while it lasted the US was a bold experiment. Sad to see it just another 'shithole country' (to quote DJT) and by any measure a Failed State.

Masks

As you can see, I'm tapping out these words whilst wearing a mask. While you, beloved reader, are reading them masked. It is more than a coincidence that we've chosen the same design favoured by our Prime Minister. The most patriotic of masks, based on the Australian flag, complete with Union Jack and Southern Cross worn, like the PM's (for some reason that entirely escapes me) upside down. This may be a reference to the notion of 'the antipodes', (i.e. the direct opposite of everything) given our upside-downness on the planet. I'd prefer to think so as it would be faintly embarrassing if the PM had simply made a mistake.

So as not to mask my intentions, today's column is about masks. And before we start let us acknowledge that the very word mask is fraught and problematic. To 'mask your intentions' is to be deceitful. Traditionally the mask hides not only one's appearance but one's true nature. Little wonder that honest decent citizens shun them, going so far as to denounce them as an attack on their sovereignty.

Before Covid people who concealed their faces were seen as sinister. You will recall Pauline Hanson wearing a burqa into Parliament to dramatise the dangers of Islam. And while today's Victorian Police might demand that you surrender your sovereignty by wearing a facial covering it seems only yesterday, they shot Ned Kelly for wearing a metallic burqua. (Of course Ned's full-metal-jacket has an ancient pedigree. In the royal sport of jousting both horse and jockey were armour-plated. Scaled down to the modern Olympics, behold the fencing mask.)

Masks were long favoured by those who share Ned Kelly's interest in bank-robbing. Few self-respecting blokes making unlawful withdrawals were seen without them. They're as important to proceedings as a sawn-off shotgun and a bag for the loot. Indeed we remember a time when banks were disinclined to welcome people wearing hoodies or crash helmets, let alone masks. Now you can't get into a supermarket, or a presidential inauguration, without one. Better still, two. 'Double masking' is the latest Covid fashion statement.

Prior to Ned K's tin hat was that poor anonymous 'Man in the Iron Mask' – forced to wear it for 34 years in French prisons including the Bastille. A lighter model mask was also mandated for another unfortunate Frenchman, the *Phantom of the Opera House*. Given the French were such trend-setters it's hardly surprising that the top French fashion houses are now producing diamond-studded masks for haute couture and pret-a-porter.

While top-to-toe masking has always been required by the KKK, In the US mask-wearing is seen by right-wing ratbags as a communist plot, reason enough to storm the Capitol and kill people. China? They're in two minds. Masks to slow the contagion of Covid are approved, even demanded. Yet they are seen as treasonable in Hong Kong where protestors seeking to slow China's pandemic of totalitarianism use masks to escape facial recognition technology.

Transformative masks are central to many a ceremonial occasion: skull masks for Mexico's Day of the Dead, carnival masks in Rio and Venice and African Fesima masks. And arguably Bali is totally a mask culture. (Margaret Mead believed that even when Balinese weren't wearing them their smiles were masks).

Who was that masked man? The Lone Ranger – with Tonto? It seems we're all masked-up now. It's a big ask to wear a mask but it may avoid a death mask.

Olden Days

I didn't expect to be around this long. Still alive and still working at 81. The one thing on which John Howard and I agree – and we were born just days apart in 1939 – is a mutual disapproval of retirement. His was forced upon him by an ungrateful electorate. I linger on.

As a free-range child of seven I didn't like my chance of making it to fourteen. The Yarra River at Kew was our playground, so cousin Terry and I regularly risked drowning. Or falling fatally from trees. Or from the horses we rode bareback in riverside paddocks. Another dangerous haunt was the storm water drain that ran below them – that we furnished with old chairs dragged from the Kew Municipal Tip. Yet here I am decades later, dodging the traffic and disease.

I belonged to the polio generation, the era of chest X-rays for TB. And now, like you, I'm contending with Corona. But the grimmest spectre of childhood came from the prospect of nuclear war. My first nickname at East Kew State, given after Hiroshima, was Adam-Bomb, but every kid knew of the nuclear threat. Not that teachers taught us to 'duck and cover' like US children. Yet the mushroom cloud was always hovering.

I made my first film during the 1960s Vietnam War, a collaboration with Bruce Petty we called *Hearts and Minds* – and vividly remember his cartoon for this newspaper showing two Vietnamese boys huddling in a burning landscape. One says to the other 'What are you going to do if you grow up.'

If. That existential word, that bleak question, was wholly applicable to kids everywhere – even in Australia – throughout the Cold War 50s and beyond, feeding into an underlying despair that gave us both nightmares and the despairing drug culture. It was like PTSD before the fact as we experienced the Third World War in instalments. Seventy years later it rages on, the Doomsday Clock remaining at one minute to midnight.

Now kids have new causes for concern. Yes, the pandemic. But there's another war, once more in slow motion, a Hot War that like the Cold War gives the young nightmares. The Climate War. Like the Cold War the dread of it reaches everywhere.

I won't be around to see if humanity and sanity win it, but the signs aren't good. In this country those signs are all pointing in the wrong direction – thanks to the war criminality of denialism, to a succession of governments that have utterly failed us. Last year's bushfires, the drought (and what is drought but a bushfire in slow motion?) are but symptoms of a far greater threat than any posed by nuclear weapons.

From mushroom clouds to skies full of smoke and ash – as half the country became Vesuvial, Pompeiin. The scale of destruction we endured or witnessed saw some humans die – along with billions of birds, animals and reptiles. Yes, billions. With more and more of our fellow creatures pushed towards extinction. And the political response? More maniacal denialism. More of the same monstrous stupidity in a parody of policy via the accelerating burning of fossil fuels.

What's the right term? Are we committing suicide? Or are we allowing ourselves to be murdered?

So let an old bloke who's been writing on the crisis for over forty years ask you this question.

What are your grandchildren going to do if they grow up?

Nostalgia Sequel

A few weeks back this page printed an inventory of things – from products to principles – that seem so past tense. From Brylcreem to hula-hoops and ministerial responsibility. Readers have responded to my list with thousands more examples and quite a few protests. My assertion that LPs have vanished was refuted with the news that business is booming. I've also learnt that there's a shop in Melbourne that stocks only one product – hula-hoops. Some old-style barbers live on, as do a few classic fish 'n chip shops. And there's a DVD rental shop in Albany WA. Rule-proving exceptions of course, but poignant.

In six decades as a columnist I've rarely seen such a response. Weeks later hundreds of funny, bittersweet and evocative emails continue to arrive, full of additions. Herewith just a few...

Salvos on the street corner. Hare Krishna on the footpaths. String bags for shopping. Free range dogs. Glass milk bottles at the door. Magpies pecking at their caps. Treadle sewing machines. Oslo lunches.

Radiograms. Box Brownies. Slide nights. Community Singing in town halls. Railway Refreshment Rooms. DDT Fly-spray. Kero heaters, kero lanterns, kero fridges. Sunday School Picnics. Home visits by the local doctor.

SP bookies – with their 'cockatoos'. Hopscotch. Treating bee-stings with Reckitt's Blue. Being woken at dawn by the neighbour's rooster, playing Cowboys and Indians, yonnie fights and quince fights, pushing hand-mowers up and down the lawn, taking newspapers to the butchers to wrap your meat order. Or selling them to the fish 'n chip shop.

Two mail deliveries per day (with the postie blowing his whistle), 'coffee' made from chicory essence, children's feet being irradiated by

X-ray machines in shoe-shops, those whooshing vacuum tubes in big retail stores, boot-makers who would 'half sole and heel' your shoes, gully traps, 'a Bex, a cup of tea and a good lie-down', F-O-R-D Pills, Ardarth, Craven A and Turf cigarettes, corsets, debutante balls, canasta, fondue dinners with copper fondue pots.

Booking interstate or international phone calls, party lines in the country, square-dancing, catching tadpoles and waiting for their legs to grow, cruelly pouring water down cicada holes to force them to the surface.

Backyard abortions. Chanting 'go back to your own country' to bewildered 'reffo' kids in the playground. Or 'Catholic dogs stink like frogs' to the kids across the street – whose response, quite fairly, was 'State State full of hate'. Ah, the good old days.

The six o'clock swill, the Rechabites Society, pub-free suburbs, Gideon bibles, typewriter ribbons, carbon paper, briquettes, lisle stockings, bed jackets, bloomers, Blue Hills, the Spirit of Progress, the Southern Aurora, red rattlers, tram conductors, fuse wire and fuse boxes, milkshakes in metal containers, steel beer cans without ring pulls that you opened with a pointed tool, signs outside plant nurseries reading AUSTRALIAN NATIVES 12/6, school desks with inkwells, making 'gings' from forks of trees, the Argonauts kids' show, When a Girl Marries, ABC announcers reading the news with BBC accents, commercial radio announcers mimicking Americans, keeping silkworms, crystal sets, mantle radios, 'getting six of the best', rotary Gestetner machines, threepences in the Christmas pud.

School Army Cadets, Porphyry Pearl, Latin classes, 'brothel creepers', Empire Day, genuine agate marbles (as opposed to tawdry 'glassies', playing 'doctors and nurses' for DIY sex education, penny bungers, Dinky toys, Meccano sets, snakes and ladders, cars without seat belts, hand signals, train guards blowing whistles, smoke and soot in the eyes from steam engines.

Rolling Jaffas down the aisle at the flicks, belly-whack dives at the local pool, 'Chinese burns' in the playground, cubby houses, playing 'statues', coming-ready-or-not, school cases, kit bags, putting pennies on the tram tracks, old toasters that opened like books, phones with round dials, playing 'jacks', Hopalong Cassidy, school bottle drives, Singers of Renown, school slates and slate pencils, fountain pens, blotting paper, cursive writing, pencils with rubber erasers on one end, secretaries taking shorthand,

The dunny man or night man (editor's note – this hero starred in many of your lists) the Rawleigh's Man, the headlight dipper-switch on the floor of the Holden, the column change, bench seats, water-operated spin-dryers, backyard incinerators, horse-and-cart rubbish collection.

Avon calling, the Twenty Pound note – aka 'the Brick' – about a week's pay for a Tradie, the Basic Wage, the guinea (one pound and one shilling), raising your hat to a woman, giving up your tram or train seat to the elderly, good manners in general, 'Esq.' after a name on an envelope.

Coolgardie safes, ice-chests, your Grocer weighing groceries before putting them in brown-paper bags, sawdust on the butcher's floor, 'spending a penny' or 'going to see a man about a horse', literally 'pulling the chain'. The chamber-pot.

Innumerable Australian colloquialisms, rhyming slang, eiderdowns, lunatic asylums, skipping ropes, ice-cream 'spiders', Tarax lemonade, the use of Mr and Mrs, the ceramic hot water bottle, the term 'tomboy', scores of names like Henry and Edna.

Wind-up cars, slot cars, pick-up sticks, tiddly-winks, kaleidoscopes, bicycle clips, whoopie cushions, practical joke shops, sherbet suckers, Vacola bottling outfits, musical chairs, pass-the-parcel, lolly fags – and 'rainbow balls' that changed colour when sucked. (You had to keep taking them out to look) All Day Suckers and sundry gobstoppers.

Choo-choo bars.

Lava lamps. Covering schoolbooks in brown paper. Leaving the plastic cover on the new lounge suite. Swan Vesta matches you struck on the sole of your shoe. Redheads in boxes made of plywood. Bonfires – and cooking spuds in the ashes. Carbide lamps. Primus stoves. Chip heaters. Hand-pump bowsers, driveway service (wash your windscreen, check your tyres). MPH. Farm windmills. Carrier pigeons. Glass scrubbing boards. Hand-wringers. Wooden pegs. Clothes props. Safari suits. Ripple-sole and blue-suede shoes. The Amateur Hour. Pick-a-Box with Bob, Dolly and Barry.

Poor peoples' food. My grandmother's specialties included fried bread and dripping on toast –and her piece-de- resistance for dessert? Nan poured boiling water on sugar-sprinkled Milk Arrowroot biscuits.

Billy tea. Zippos. Basin haircuts. Walking to school in all weathers. Learning the times table, the smell of phenyl, the taste of castor oil, banks open Saturday mornings, cheque books, spinning tops, aerograms, telegrams, protractors, junket, Post, Pix and People magazines, Sunbathers nudist mag with air-brushed blurs of the naughty bits, Clag, womens' gloves, Westerns. Duffel coat. Army Disposal Shops.

Coles Funny Picture Book. John Martins in Adelaide. Glomesh handbags. Blue rinses. Feather beds. Three Stooges. Elocution lessons. Police whistles. Peashooters. The whistling kettle.

We were deeply touched by a letter from Michelle... 'I live in a Retirement Village with (much) older people, We have a regular cuppa-n chat. It's a challenge with deafness, Asperger's, women who have lived a life suppressed. But with your article we had a terrific walk down memory lane and I was able to get each and everyone involved.'

Hope you've found it therapeutic too. Thanks for your help.

Ghost Story

Ghost: the soul, spirit or spectre of a dead person that appears to the living. I don't believe in ghosts yet acknowledge they exist. In ever growing numbers. Thanks, for better or worse, to the movies.

Cut to the façade of Sydney's State Theatre some decades ago. Dissolve to the interior. Slow pan to reveal it's a Full House. Zoom to the stage. Cut to a two-shot of two men sharing a lectern, one rather portly, the other very tall. We are witnessing the opening ceremony of the Sydney Film Festival, with Adams and James Stewart cutting the ribbon.

Time lapse. Five minutes later the pair take side-by-side seats in the balcony. The lights go down. The curtains part. A film begins. Hitchcock's *Rear Window* starring James Stewart and Grace Kelly. Cut to reaction shot of Stewart who murmurs 'haven't seen this in twenty years'. He is watching the ghost of Grace Kelly. And a ghost of himself at 50.

Cut to my reaction shot to his reaction. Cut to XCU of Stewart. His expression is troubled, unhappy.

James Stewart was the Tom Hanks of his era – and a very long era it was. Like Tom today James was the official US good guy, starring in such historical upbeat films as Capra's *Mr Smith Goes To Washington* and *It's A Wonderful Life*, Cukor's *The Philadelphia Story*, in Ford's 'Westerns' and a cluster of other Hitchcock thrillers like *Vertigo*. With few exceptions Stewart chose to play heroes, patriots, men of character and decency. Like Hanks, he was Mr. America.

Cut to 2021. He and Hitchcock are long dead, as is most of the *Rear Window* cast and a majority of those who saw the film on its release in 1954. But thanks to the motion picture, movie stars never die. They haunt our imaginations and may well outlive the cinemas, now ghosts of their former selves. Ghostly, glamorous presences in Technicolour, Vista-Vision and Netflix.

These days we revive the dead in other ways, with necrophilic 'biopics' about Judy Garland, Marilyn Monroe, and now, thanks to his exhumation by Baz Luhrmann, Elvis Presley.

Thus cinema is a vast cemetery where the unquiet dead rise from the grave as required. No resting in peace for stars, particularly those who died young and tragically. And we must be thankful for it. We measure our lives in movies as surely we do with music, and in Australia it remains mainly American movies (they don't call Hollywood 'the dream factor' for nothing) and American music born in Tin Pan Alley, in Memphis, on Broadway.

(All those telly series about zombies – we seem to prefer our entertainers deceased.)

Unlove Letters

The Gyngell name will remind the younger reader of David, the TV executive who, having long been James Packer's bestie, had a brutal brawl with him on a Bondi footpath. But older readers may recall his father Bruce, famously credited as 'the first face to appear on Australian TV'. After helping Sir Frank Packer establish TCN9 Bruce decamped to the UK becoming aide-de-camp to the to the le grand fromage of British broadcasting, Lord Grade, aka 'Low Grade Lew'.

On a London visit, after a business meeting with Lew, I renewed my friendship with Bruce who told proud he'd been when his powerful employer entrusted him to open his personal mail, only later realising that Lew was afraid of letter bombs. As were many at the time as around the world they were blowing up in their recipients' faces. Other letters contained anthrax or, in one memorable case for your columnist, a turd in Gladwrap, delivered in mint condition by Australia Post.

I was used to envelopes from the public containing insults and even death threats but this was a new experience. I thought about passing it on to the police, but their ballistic skills stopped with bullets. But I have my suspicions as to the source.

Sandra, my long-time secretary, always feared opening my mail – and not just because it might contain anthrax or excrement. So on receipt of a heavy and mysterious parcel she tossed it in my Paddington swimming pool. When Sandra deemed it safe I scooped it out. It contained my annual allotment of homemade marmalade from Simonette, a beloved reader.

A year late terrorism was at its height. We'd had the Red Guard, the Unabomber, with 'single purpose' terrorists targeting US abortion clinics. And topping the list and death toll, 9/11. So when a large parcel for me arrived at the ABC the mailroom deemed it so suspicious that the entire Ultimo HQ was evacuated, hundreds mustered out to wait anxiously in Harris Street. Everyone from the bureaucrats above to the babies in the crèche.

The mailroom staff was particularly troubled by the way my address was written, so clearly resembling the calligraphy of Bin Laden. Thus the bomb squad was called. Unlike the US, no lumbering tank-like vehicle arrived with men dressed in bomb resistant HAZMAT costumes radio-controlling purpose-built robots. Just a Falcon from the local cop shop. Two young cops emerged, poked at the parcel with their boots, lugged it to the Falcon and chucked it into the boot. Then and only then could the hundreds of staff return to their TV and radio shows, much shaken by their narrow escape.

I was blissfully ignorant of all this, busy in Paddington dictating replies to that week's hate mail. I had a lifelong policy of answering letters, even obscene ones from the anonymous. (That might sound tricky but often would-be anonymous correspondents, out of habit, put their names and address on the back of the envelope.) When finally alerted to the goings-on at Ultimo I felt a strange surge of patriotism. No overblown theatrics (though that's probably an unfortunate choice of adjective). Just two kids in a cop car.

A few hours passed until we heard the denouement. The parcel had contained jars of Simonette's most excellent marmalade. Remembering Sandra's concerns at Paddo she'd sent her jam to the ABC.

No, I never ever got my marmalade back. But no complaints. Hope the police enjoyed it. They deserved it.

Public Libraries

The East Kew Sub-branch of the Kew Municipal Library, occupying a repurposed church hall a few miles from the tiny farm where I lived with my grandparents, was also connected, over vast stretches of time and space, to the fabled library in Oxford founded in 1444 by Thomas Bodley. Also to libraries founded four centuries earlier by the Fatimid Caliph Al-Akim – and to early American examples kindled by Benjamin Franklin. We're talking the long history of a one of civilisations best ideas. Australia's first? The Melbourne Public Library – now the State Library of Victoria – in 1856.

From the age of eight Gran and Grandpa entrusted me with a weekly visit to the Sub-branch to borrow 'one romance and a mystery' for them and a William or *Biggles* for me. Until I knew the oeuvres of Richmal Crompton and Capt. W. C. Johns by heart – along with all the books by Mary Grant Bruce and the *Seven Little Australians.*

Then the librarian took pity on me and invited me, to step up into the grown-ups section. Both a literary and a literal step. For me as significant as Armstrong's onto the Moon. Then, in a prescient moment, she handed me the book that would change my life forever. John Steinbeck's *The Grapes of Wrath.* Five years later I'd left Eltham High and became an under-age member of the Communist Party. One year later, at the age of 16, I was the youngest Australian to have an ASIO file. Thankyou librarian. Thankyou Steinbeck.

For four decades I've earned a living interviewing authors. Now their 'signed copies', numbers swelled the books sent by hopeful writers or publishers, fill half-a-dozen rooms and two purpose-built buildings here on the farm. A guesstimate? At least 40,000 – including early editions of

Williams and *Biggles*.

Though I no longer need to borrow from the local libraries – and Scone and Muswellbrook have fine ones – and though told physical books of actual paper are in decline – I visit the fine examples in Scone and Muswellbrook to pay homage to (drum roll) the very notion of the Public Library. Public is, of course, an unfashionable adjective – as the endless attacks on public ownership attest. Public broadcasting, public health, public roads, public education. There was even an organised attack on the public toilet. If it walks or stands still privatise it.

But not, I beg you, the public library. In the US they provide not merely books and computer access but a place for the homeless to huddle. Here they remain, along with public parks, one of the few surviving public spaces. Giving access to wisdom, information and a sense of community.

The book – in the form of the codex – began to replace the scroll from the time of Julius Caesar. Now, ironically, with various form of E book, we're back to scrolling. But bound pages of paper will survive and outlive the decimal usurpers. I love the look of them, the feel of them, even the smell of them.

Looking back through the mists of time and macular degeneration to the East Kew Sub-branch of the Kew Municipal Library I wish I knew the name of the librarian so I could lobby for some sort of posthumous gong.

And I wish I'd salvaged that little wooden step for posterity – and donated it in to the National Library in her memory.

My first step into reading grown-up books. And my first step into life as a left-wing looney.

Philip

When I saw the headline PHILIP DEAD AT 99 I thought, for a dreadful moment, that it was me. Had being denied a jab aged me a few years and proved fatal?

Fortunately I detected some signs of life, including a faint pulse and a hint of mist on a mirror held to the nostrils. Then with a sigh of relief (another symptom of continued existence) realised it was another Philip who'd gone from bucket list to bucket kicking, Phil the Greek. Two-paces-behind-Phil. Consort of the Queen, father of Charles, hero of Tony Abbott. Philip with one l.

E.G. Whitlam, that classic classicist, always scored his nib through one of my l's when before signing a letter, explaining on more than one occasion that Phillip was an abomination, that only Philip should be used as a prenom. 'Phillip is, at best, a surname,' Gough would say with a fastidious shudder.

Staying with the Greeks for another moment the name Philip has to do with horses. Not to be confused with Pharlap, Philip apparently means 'lover of horses' which is not the case in my case. Great lumbering dangerous brutes. Was fond of Blossom as a child, the Clydesdale Grandpa used for ploughing. But attempts to master horse-riding forty years later on my farm failed. I didn't need to be bucked off. I'd just fall off. And thought Elmswood's been home to many a horse owned by family or staff I opted for the mechanical alternative, the quad-bike.

It's a bit mean of God not to let Phil the Greek do the ton. Another few days and he'd have qualified for a telegram from his horse-loving missus. (That's if they still send centenarians congratulatory telegrams from the Palace. (These days it's probably a Royal tweet or a Facebook post). 99 years is, as they say, a good innings, but as any test cricketer would agree it's not like scoring a century. Would it have hurt someone to fiddle the books? Demand a recount? OK, OK, a 41-gun salute here in the colonies is not to be sneezed at, unless you have Covid.

And Phil had lots of Australian connections other that trudging behind HM on antipodean Royal Tours. I knew two of his Australian girlfriends – the first a mutual friend, recently deceased, who whilst not a lover of horses was certainly a lover of Phil's. The other paramour was the partner of an Australian portrait painter who giggled that she and PTG had performed in close proximity to the Royal Throne. The actual physical throne, not a metaphor

(Philip's extracurricular activities were, of course, nudge-nudge-wink-winked at in *The Crown*. And in a biography, most notoriously Kitty Kelley's unauthorised *The Royals*, where she gave him similar treatment to previous kiss-and-tells on Sinatra and JFK. Of course we're talking minor peccadillos, not major scandals like uncle Edward's love affair with Hitler or son Andrew's involvement with Epstein and Ghislaine.)

Also confusing the issue of who'd actually died on the day of the PHILIP DEAD AT 99 headline was the story someone tweeted to your columnist about a namesake Phillip (two l's) Adams in the US. Published by Associated Press the story, dated the very day of the Duke's demise, read in part... 'The coroner announced that the brain of Phillip Adams will be tested for a degenerative disease that has shown to cause violent mood swings'.

Having narrowly survived the death of the Duke here I am enduring an autopsy, what Hercule Poirot called 'my little grey cells' being placed under the microscope. Then I read on... Phillip Adams was an NRL player who'd morphed into a mass murderer.

Vale Philip. But not Phillip.

Birthdays

John Howard and I have always been close. At least when it comes to birthdays. We were both born in July just a few days apart in 1939. Just apart enough to give us different astrological ID's – me a Cancer, he a Leo. Thus saving the ancient pseudoscience considerable embarrassment.

And who wants the Cancer as his/her sign? It's more of a death sentence. 'Jimmy Dancer' in rhyming slang, the cosmic crab all too often sends one tap-dancing to an early demise – although I speak as a cancer survivor. But there's one thing that inevitably leads to death: the incurable birthday. Symbolised by the cake with its fatal fossil-fuel candles.

As I've grown older I've shunned the birthday cake. The sugary icing can trigger a diabetic debacle while the candles add to global emissions. Particularly in the case of John Howard and me as fellow octogenarians. Yes, it's been a while since John was a Young Liberal. Appropriately candlelit cakes would be illegal during bushfire season and neither John nor I have enough puff to blow out all that candlepower. We'd have to get one of those infernal leaf-blower things.

Which is another reason I forget peoples' birthdays. I recently had to send an apologetic email to youngest daughter Aurora, who lives in Paris doing left-wing things, for forgetting hers. As I pointed out this annual lapse of memory – and it applies to the birthdays of all four daughters – derives from my desperation to forget my birthday. A classic case of repressed memory. With the birthday cake representing a funeral pyre, I do not wish to have one. I encourage everyone to forget mine – the birthday as well as the sponge. Yet the only birthday I want is the next one. And the next. Etcetera. Ad nauseam. Birthdays that rage against Dylan Thomas's 'dying of the light'.

Which brings us to 'Happy Birthday', the most tuneless of dirges with its woeful lyrics. It makes Handel's Death March sound chirpy. There's nothing remotely happy about Happy Birthday, the only song that's even more miserable than God Save the Queen. I suspect the same composer wrote both of them having forgotten to take his anti-depressants. Along with that heart-breaking woe-is-us song sung on the birthdays of actual years.

I defy anyone to hear Happy Birthday to You, God Save the Queen and Auld Lang Syne without wanting to phone Philip Nitschke. And who is this old Lang Syne? Is he related to old Lang Hancock?

(And I should point out that HM doesn't seem to like her cake and candles either – celebrating her Queens Birthday on the wrong day)

Birthday, deathday. Let me commend a little song from an early Disney version of *Alice in Wonderland.* Walt's lyrics began thus. 'A very merry unbirthday to you'. Much better, and appropriate to the other 364 days of the year.

To add to the confusion the Chinese calculate age from the time of conception – a bit like the anti-abortionists in the Roman Catholic Church. And racehorses all have their birthdays on the same day. As does Australia Day, though that birthday is increasingly contested by ungrateful First Nations folk.

Hence my idea, launched this very day in 2021, to cancel all birthdays. Australia's, the Queen's, the Year's and yours. By banishing birthdays we'll immediately feel younger. Don't worry – you could still get presents, but on a less bureaucratised basis.

It's bipartisan. John Howard joins me in the recommendation.

Frontline

Shortly after Australia had gone wandering from Gondwanaland, young Rupert Murdoch founded a newspaper of the same name and its first editor; the self-effacing Max Newton hired its first television critic. As Rupert had no television interests at the time there'd be no need to be two-faced, yet the critic chose anonymity behind the pseudonym Janus, the two-faced Roman god. Now it can be revealed that Janus (or J. Anus those on the receiving end of his tirades called him) was Andrew Denton's dad Kit.

On Denton's retirement, the third editor in rapid succession – the prescient Adrian Deamer – hired a young Adams in his stead. It was my turn to lacerate those guilty of televisual sins. Naturally one of my first targets was Frontline, the new 'public affairs' program fronted by a clown called Mike Moore, a low-rent version of Ray Current Affair Martin. If that was possible.

This was tabloid television at its worst, and you can't get worster than that. Night after night journalistic ethics were flouted. Readers of a certain age will recall *Frontline*'s track record. Foot-in-the door bullying. Hidden camera lurking. Reputation destruction. Cash for commentary. Endless puff pieces with 'product placement'. Remember Moore's dangerous interview with a crazed gunman holding kids as hostages? I know the police were infuriated – as was the late Mike Willessee who regarded this episode as 'outrageously reckless'.

With the help of his disreputable and egomaniacal colleagues Brooke Vandenburg and Martin di Stasio Moore and his succession of EP's (trade talk for Executive Producers, aka Enormous Penises) denigrated the young unemployed ('bludgers') and Aboriginals ('drunks') while providing a platform for bigots. You may recall Moore's 'interview' with a young Pauline Hanson.

When not marketing moral panics, punctuated with mawkish sentimentality to show the 'soft side' of Moore, scientists were derided and the 'dangers of vaccinations' trumpeted. Soft targets – people who couldn't defend themselves were excoriated whilst the Mr. Bigs were ignored. Particularly if they were friends of the network owners. Fake news? *Frontline* invented it.

And all the time the program pretended to care for 'the battlers' for whom it had nothing but contempt. Yes, the Press Council were constantly ticking them off, but the EP's just pissed themselves laughing. Moore characterised himself as the Velvet Fist or some such (in contrast to Yana's 'perfumed bulldozer) and the show showed there were always deeper depths to sink to. Snakes' bellies to be beneath.

Forgive my outburst but it's all come rushing back because of Netflix. Sadly people are now binge-viewing old *Frontlines* eps. Over thirty of them. Showing how the defecations of these tabloid terrorists won the ratings, making Moore one of the highest paid presenters (and Logie winners) in TV history. Second only to Ray Martin.

I've been talking about *Frontline* with some old friends who shared my distaste – nay, disgust! – Rob Sitch and Jane Kennedy. How could the Control Board, the Press Council and the Australian Journalists Association have let this happen? Let it continue? Even worse, if not worster, Moore, di Stasio and Vandenberg were recently elevated to the Media Hall of Fame – and Mike now guest lectures in Media Studies at the UNSW.

Rob, Jane, Santo, Tom and Michael – co founders of Working Dog – are thinking of doing a satire on *Frontline* after the next series of *Utopia*. But how do you satirise something beyond satire? And mightn't it run the risk of giving this sort of television the oxygen of publicity?

Goya

Though an Antipodean atheist I made regular pilgrimages when visiting London or Madrid to genuflect before my two favourite artists. I'd take a taxi to the Tate to gaze in wonderment at the golden canvasses of Turner. In Madrid, it was straight to the Prado, to be awestruck by the black paintings of Goya.

Though they were born and died a few years apart (Goya 1746-1828, Turner 1775-1851) and ignorant of each other's work, both dominated the cultural lives of their countries. Both began life in the respectable, middle-class and both would die unrespectable deaths. Yet the two geniuses were very different – Turner reclusive and eccentric, Goya at the centre of things, simultaneously social critic and social climber.

Turner was primarily a painter of English landscapes, Goya a painter of Spanish nightmares. One enthralled by storms at sea, the other by storms of human emotion, by the disasters of war and revolution.

Turner and Goya shared a comparable daring of expression and bold theatricality. No static 'still lives' for them. No tidy, timid bowls of fruit, no flattering, complacent portraits. They depicted their different worlds with artistic and personal courage.

I'm writings these words in the company of Turner and Goya etchings and two paintings. I found my tiny Turner in a Melbourne junk shop almost 60 years ago – an oil sketch for the View of Orvieto, hanging in the Tate. The etchings? Only mass-produced hints of his great seascapes. But the Goyas! A full-scale Portrait of a Madrid matron purchased at Sotheby's 50 years ago – categorized by that snootiest auctioneer as 'painted in whole or part' by the master. I wasn't disappointed when she emerged from the claustrophobia of her crate, blinking in the bright Australian light, though the woman I look at most days is, let it be said, a charmless grump, her portrait candid to the point of cruelty.

I also have 24 Goya etchings from the Caprichos. Decades ago Kerry Packer asked me to write for *The Bulletin*, for the preceding century home to many famous political cartoonists. So it seemed appropriate that I demand payment in cartoons. But only Goya's, and only first editions.

A puzzled Packer agreed. For two years a Goya etching would arrive every month. They now frame the Madrid matron in a farmhouse almost as remote from Sydney as it is from Spain. I like to think Francisco would be amused.

Later Spain would be home to famous surrealists – few with a scintilla of Goya's graphic gifts, his preposterous fantasizing. In this regard Goya has the phantasmagoric fecundity of Bosch, one that dwarfs Dali's. The theatricality we see in the Black Paintings scaled down, yet losing little of the power to confront.

I think Freud would agree that the interpretation of Goya's images is as problematic as the interpretation of dreams. Though I've seen them up close and personal for much of my long life, they remain mysterious.

When it comes to virtuosity only Picasso belongs in Goya's company; his *Guernica*, painted in reaction to the Nazis' bombing of the Spanish city, comparable in scale and horror to Goya's response to the revolution and the invasion by Napoleon.

Choosing exile from Spain in 1924, Goya's health further deteriorated, his work became even darker and angrier. No 'happy ever after' here. Goya raged against the dying of his light.

So he's good company for an old man who shares much of his deafness and, I hope, some of his defiance. No longer able to make my pilgrimage, I thank the Prado for lending him to our NGV.

In the Beginning

What is your earliest memory? Think back. Not to a fond family anecdote told about your childhood. Not to something kindled by leafing through a photo album. But to a memory of your very own, a memory you actually own.

Perhaps a face looking down at you in the pram? Being tossed aloft by a playful father? Frightened by a dog?

My first memory remains as vivid in 2021 at it was in 1940. I can date it accurately because I'd just learned to walk and in 1941 my father would leave us to be a padre in the Australian Army in New Guinea. I have his wartime dairies on the desk, cramped writing complaining about how indifferent soldiers were to him and his religion.

The memory: I am toddling as fast as tiny legs will carry me, terrified by the fact that the sky is on fire. I manage to wrench open a flywire back door and rush through darkness into a brightly lit room.

Years later I could decode it – I was witnessing my first thunderstorm, running beneath the row of peppercorns beside the house. The Congregational Manse in Maryborough, Victoria, where the Rev Charles Adams was the vicar, possibly interrupting him in the preparation of a sermon. Mother Sylvia plays no part in the memory. Neither parent recalled the incident – so it's not a story that's been passed on.

The church, the manse and the peppercorns were still there thirty years later when I returned to Maryborough for the first time in my late twenties. Probably all gone now – few Congo's seem to have survived the upheaval of the 'uniting church' era.

My father has been dead for decades. He was expelled from the ministry after the war (for, it seems, being drunk at the pulpit) but had lost his faith long before losing his job. I recall him bitterly describing the clerical collar as 'a whitewashed wall around a lunatic asylum'.

For a few years I'd begin my radio programs by asking the good and the great what I'm now asking you. 'What is your first memory'. It was hardly a way to relax them – most were confused and discomforted by the question. But after a pause a few answered the question with certainty – and unsurprisingly it often involved trauma.

Nannette Dutton, wife of historian Geoffrey Dutton and a formidable writer herself, had a memory similar to mine. Yes, a storm! Lots of thunder and lightning. But rather than rushing to her father for protection she remembers being swept up in his arms – and held exultantly aloft. Whereas my experience would presage a lifelong preoccupation with the apocalyptic (well timed for the Cold War) Nannette recalls being, in effect, charged with optimism.

While first memories don't seem to have attracted much academic attention, a few studies suggest that about 40% of us date them to around 2 years of age. Many are fabrications, family fictions, and it is doubtful brain development permits memories much earlier. (It's something to do with the hippocampus – so let's leave prenatal memories out of it).

But I would be fascinated to hear from you about yours. Who knows? We might get another collaborative column out of it – to match your marvellous outpouring of memories of things going going gone that required a double-page spread in the magazine.

Please remember this... my preferred email address is philadams@ozemail.com.au. Snail mail very welcome. To me at Elmswood, Gundy. 2337. I also accept mental telepathy.

First Memories

Offering a traumatic 'first memory' of my own I asked readers to send me theirs. Not some 'photographic memory' from an ancient Kodak, or a family heirloom. But a genuine personal memory. To say I was overwhelmed by the response – in both quantity and quality – is an understatement. To accommodate them would not only fill our magazine to overflowing but could crowd out the pages of the entire newspaper. A majority were views from playpen, pram, pushchair and, surprisingly, the potty. Many an octogenarian and nonagenarian reader remembered experiences from the blitz in London – others all-time horrors witnessed in Germany. As expected, a majority were dramatic or traumatic, reflections from readers born into conflicts around the world or in the nursery. Many could be attributed to Hitler but others to the arrival of an unwanted baby brother or sister. And the first memory of others involved their parents' reaction to the Kennedy assassination. They're still arriving by email, mail and twitter. Today, a sampling. Next weekend a double-page spread.

1940. I'm four. Air-raid sounds herald the indomitable Luftwaffe. The drone of Heinkels gets louder, the room lights up with flashes and the steady crump crump of explosions. The all-clear wails. We were enjoying the son et lumiere – unaware of the total destruction and death two streets away.

Around 1937, I'm four, in a south London suburb. An old man – he must have been a doctor – lays me out on an ironing board. I'm made to inhale chloroform. I later learn I'd had my adenoids (?) removed.

I was two. I'm standing in front of Grandma, singing or babbling. I remember being pulled aside. Dad and his two brothers carry Grandpa away. He'd had a heart attack and died. It's my second Christmas, Tasmania, World War II in the background. Toys restricted. My sister has a pre-war China doll. I expect to receive one. What I get is a home-made rag doll with a papier mache face. I stand up very still in my cot and hurl the thing across the room. I never saw the doll again.

Glasgow, 1939. I'm three years old. The Clyde shipyards are targets for the German bombers. Loud air-raid sirens going off and my mother shouting, 'Arthur, get Mickey, we're going to the cellar.' The Mickey? My Mickey Mouse gasmask. No recollection of what happened thereafter but I knew I was safe if Mickey was with me.

The 1950s, I'm around two. Dad took me outside and I remember him kneeling beside me whilst I gazed with absolute wonder and joy at the dark blue night sky. My father then threw a tennis ball into the sky – I see it soaring but didn't see it come down! Like all such memories, it's not the actual event but the feeling that stays with you forever. I was born in Sydney, 1948. My earliest memory is of colour and indistinctive movement which eventually consolidated into the vague image of one of the world's greatest inventions, the Hills Hoist.

I am Max, 83 years old. Born in Glebe Point in 1937. Guy Fawkes night and Dad had a box of crackers. One of the fireworks jumped into the box and the whole lot went off with great amounts of smoke and money. I remember being terrified and running into the house, watching the chaos through the front window.

I was born in Hawthorn, Melbourne in 1945. I vividly recall my first words as I waddled down the hall to the comfort of my parents' bed, uttering my first words, 'Bring own piddow.' Is my intention to repeat those words to Our Dear Lord on arrival in the next life.

My earliest memory, clearly etched, is sitting in a tub on our kitchen table having a bath. I remember standing up in a cot. My mother was being followed around by a very noisy Electrolux sausage vacuum cleaner.

I was three years old when my brother Paul was born and I cried and cried. I wanted a sister.

1957, two years old, we had travelled from Scotland to Libya and the capital Tripoli. Reunited with my father! I must have had some recollection of him even at that young age, some sense of comfort about the man who picked me up in his arms on our arrival.

I'm 87. My first memories go back to my late 2s and 3s. I have a vision of standing on the footpath when a small dog came running out of the greengrocer's and bit me on the leg.

I date my first unmediated memory to the 23rd November 1963, at just after 6pm. I see my Dad in his usual chair watching the News. He had a look on his face I had never seen before on any human face. This chronically taciturn and repressed man looked at me and said, 'The President's dead.'

I'm a babe in arms, apparently being held by my mother. There is a stench – in front of me a large trellis with animal skins pegged out to dry. Perhaps rabbit skins. Many years later my mother said, 'You couldn't possibly have remembered this. It was at Uncle Charlie's farm in Bull's Brook.'

Like you, my first memory is of a thunderstorm. I'm three or four, at my grandmother's flat in Randwick, and lightning and thunder had me cowering under the table. There is an accompanying smell of 'worstle' – thin beef sausages – and sauerkraut.

I was born in Brunswick in 1934. During the war slit-trenches had been dug in nearby Premier's Park to shelter citizens when the threat of Japanese bombers seemed to be real.

I was born in England in 1943. During the first quarter of 1945 a

V1 flying bomb, destined for London, crashed and exploded near our home on the Surrey/Sussex border. Most of the windows were shattered and glass fragments ricocheted around the bedroom. I was struck by a shard of glass, leaving me with a dark indentation in my palm. I remember intense and terrifying noise accompanied by flashes of light that seemed to last for minutes and left me wailing.

The year is 1954 and I'm in love for the first time. I would lie on the bed dreaming of her. Her name was Christina Reilly, my kindergarten teacher. I still miss her 66 years later.

My father takes me to Maylan's Aerodrome in Perth to see Kingsford Smith land. Our interest in aviation would take a dramatic turn when my father died in the ANA crash in 1950 – Australia's largest commercial crash at the time.

I'm admitted to the Women and Children's Hospital in Adelaide in 1952. For my first injection of penicillin. Over the next eight months I would have five one day and eight the next at all hours. It was the middle of the polio epidemic. The ward was filled with children, many prisoners of iron lung machines. To this day I am still scared of the dark.

The aroma of burning pinewood takes me back to Yanko in 1959 as a four-y-o. A woman was burning rubbish in her backyard and the crackle of the fire and the willowy plumes of smoke curling upwards into a blue morning sky. The aroma remains singularly alluring to me.

I was a very little girl and my father would put me on the kitchen table and cane me. I don't remember why. I cried so much. My father demanded that I stop. I couldn't so he resumed caning me. In the background my mother's voice saying, 'John, no, please stop. Please.' He didn't. I'm 76 now and can still hear my mother's voice.

I'm 80. I remember being pushed around in a pram thinking 'how good is this' or words to that effect. The feeling of being looked after has stuck in my memory all this time.

I was born in London in 1932. At the age of four I remember seeing the Crystal Palace being burnt down.

I'm a 1960s child. My first memory is sitting on the back steps with my grandfather. He'd been in the war in New Guinea and cried at night in his sleep. He died of emphysema when he was only 60. I miss him still.

A quiet suburban street in Melbourne. My mother on the porch breastfeeding my baby brother. I sit beside her, two years old, breastfeeding my dolly. My father steps outside 'Kennedy's been shot.' 'Oh no,' cried my mother. Black and white images flashed across the TV screen.

I was born in December 1939. My parents lived in a house in Mosman just up the street from Cape Curlew where Streeton and his artist mates used to camp out. I remember our windows being boarded up at night, covered with cardboard and paper to prevent any light from getting out. I remember one night two big booming explosions coming from somewhere in the distance. It would have been a Japanese midget submarine attack. I thought it was all rather exciting but my parents were really scared – having just escaped Hitler's Austria.

Belfast, 1946. I'm three or four years old. Playing in the street among the air-raid shelters. An ambulance arrives. We all run after it. It stops outside my house. My mother comes out on a stretcher. I still remember the silence. Turns out Mum had diphtheria. She survives.

I seem to be in a pram and can hear the sound of tennis balls. I learn later it was on a lawn court. Sounds first, visuals later.

My earliest memories involve nuns. We were poor and they'd look after me while my Mum went to work. It was in a convent somewhere near Eastwood where the nuns grew their own vegetables. One day we were helping pick watermelons. I kept being bitten by ants.

My earliest memory is of course crystalline snow heaped on a solid corner strainer post of a section of wire fence on Gran's farm in the Mitta Valley. There was a strong suspicion that Mum suffered from post-natal depression and as my father was the teacher at Everton across in the Oven's Valley, we often stayed at the farm. I also remember an outside dunny covered in bougainvillea.

Sherlock Jones

For the past few months, thanks to his amanuensis Dr. Watson and his lifelong fan Stephen Fry, my five-hour commutes betwixt Sydney and the Bush have been in the fascinating company of the world's most famous detective (sorry Hercule) Mr Sherlock Holmes. Fry has recorded the entire oeuvre of Conan Doyle and I'm only halfway through the longest-ever audiobook.

Current case? *The Hound of the Baskervilles.* No spoilers please.

The story is particularly interesting as the only Holmes' cases that seems to involve the supernatural, though Sherlock, the supreme rationalist, is intent on proving otherwise. Time will tell.

But here's the paradox. Conan Doyle himself was literally 'away with the fairies'. (Check the famous 1917 mystery of the Cottingley Fairies in which Sir Arthur was gulled by two naughty little girls with fake photos taken at the bottom of the garden). And during that boom time of fraudulent 'spiritualists' with table-rappings, messages from the dead and 'ectoplasm' issuing from mouths and sometimes vaginas, Conan Doyle was the most gullible of men.

Abandoning Holmes' forensic logic there seemed nothing too unbelievable for Doyle to believe. When friend Harry Houdini tried to save Doyle from himself – by replicating all the mediums' conjuring tricks – Arthur refused to accept the evidence. He accused Harry of possessing supernatural powers and only pretending to be an illusionist.

When Sir Arthur wasn't belting out his brilliant Baker St best-sellers he wrote a score of books endorsing the bogus.

I now realise that my oldest friend, Barry Jones, has a similarly bifurcated brain. The supremely sceptical Minister for Science is also drawn to that other world. I could do a Dr Watson on any number of cases wherein I've seen him sorely tempted by 'the other side'. On journeys together we've revisited places – like his identification of an alternative burial place for Mozart. Brushing aside my alternative explanation Barry insists this event is beyond rational explanation.

A few days later, when boarding a Boeing to leave Vienna, Barry stopped dead – overwhelmed by a premonition of doom. I shoved him through the doorway. We didn't crash. Score one for the skeptic.

Whilst we joined together as skeptics in denouncing the fad for Nostradamus' quatrains in the 60s and 70s – did a telly show together trying to show how people were being hoaxed. Yet I remember him hiring a water diviner during a Melbourne drought. And his being persuaded by St Malachy's 'the Prophecy of the Popes' – something else you might check out in Wikipedia.

And let it be said Barry has long been tempted by the ultimate supernaturalism of the Roman Catholic Church to which for decades I've expected him to convert. On the trip we took for John Gorton when putting together a joint plan to revive our film industry I'd oft see him heading for the gloomiest cathedrals to kneel on the coldest flagstones to pray.

As a co-founder of the Australian Skeptics I part company with my bestie on all the above, though we're in agreement on most matters scientific, political, cultural and secular. When discussing this dilemma decades ago Barry explained that his variation on parallel universes came 'from different parts of my brain'.

So be it. Like Sir Arthur's Barry's brain is big enough to contain a cornucopia of contradictions. Approaching his ninth decade Barry's brain remains bountiful, a work in progress, his beliefs evolving. I must ask Stephen Fry to turn Sherlock Jones' writings into an even longer audiobook.

Art Critics

Some people take art criticism a little too far. Take the Taliban's 2001 dynamiting of that most monumental of monuments – the 6th century Bamiyan Buddhas. Or ISIS in 2015, damaging every ancient statue they could find – including the Winged Bull of Nineveh. Not well educated in either good manners or artistic matters ISIS took time off to from beheading humans to decapitating mere plaster casts in captured museums.

Statues of limitations. Remember the toppling of Saddam Hussein's monstrous statue in Firdos Square? Neither a great loss to art history nor a recent development. Egyptian pharaohs regularly defaced (literally the faces) of predecessors. And imagine the vast junkyards in Russia that must exist to house redundant sculptures of Lenin, Stalins? They went to the scrap yard decades before – more serried ranks of them than China's 'Entombed Warriors'. Meanwhile, in London's Highgate Cemetery, the looming sculpture of Karl Marx has suffered a few bombings. I suspect Gerard Henderson.

If so, Gerard may have been inspired by fellow citizen Lazlo Toth. A Hungarian-born Australian Lazlo was a geologist by trade who, extrapolating from a lifetime spent banging at rocks with a hammer, entered the Vatican in 1972 and proceeded to do a Whelan-the-Wrecker on Michelangelo's Pieta. Took decades to repair, as did poor mad Lazlo. He died in Sydney in 2012.

Not that the Vatican should complain, given its own record in attacking scores of statues in its collection. As I've reported previously in a huge inside job every classical nude – Greek and Roman – had it penis hammered off in an orgy of prudery. The wounds were emphasised rather than concealed with crudely affixed plaster fig leaves – the maimed members now locked in a chest in the Vatican vaults. Seems the Catholic Church has some problems with human sexuality.

Madame Tussaud's has handled historical changes with tact. When a celebrity runs out of time his/her head is recycled. The wax is melted down and, lo and behold, it morphs into a new model. The same could be done with bronze.

Stone is more problematic. Bigger than Bamiyan's Buddhas are Mt. Rushmore's presidents – and it wouldn't have been surprising had Trump issued an ultimatum: 'Add me to it or I'll blow it up'. All will be revealed in a new book by another disenchanted member of Donald's dilapidated dynasty

In the Failed State of the US, still haemorrhaging from its Civil Wars, there've been countless battles royal over Jubilation T. Cornpone statues of Confederate heroes. Black Lives Matter have led huge protests against statues of racists and slave-owners from the Deep South to London – and even in Oxford University dignified rioters demanded the toppling of imperialist Cecil Rhodes.

Locally the issue has been too many Cooks spoiling our historic broth – with increasingly frequent attacks on effigies of the English explorer. There's a few Cookies I'd like to de-pedestal, but for a different reason. Quite part from the pain they cause many indigenous Australians, they're artistically offensive. Clunky, crappy statues that should be banned. If not Talibanned. I make no comment on the new bronze of Lady Di.

P.S. It seems political leaders are better off being preserved in embalming fluid than bronze. Look at Lenin, still drowsing in Red Square, at Mao in Tiananmen and Ho in Hanoi. I'm crowdfunding a plan to embalm our current crop. Immediately. Meanwhile the National Portrait Gallery is switching from paintings to picklings.

Signatures

The Sebel Town House in Sydney, like the Chelsea in New York, had a long association with there's-no-business-like-show-business. Of modest size and unpretentious appearance it fell well short of *****. Yet it was the preferred address of touring rock bands, thespians and some resident eccentrics.

There was forever a group of kids on the footpath hopefully holding autograph books. So when the owners were pondering a new name for their restaurant I suggested Signatures.

With The Sebel my Sydney home I took it for granted you'd share a lift with John Cleese. Or in the event of a (false) fire alarm at 3am find yourself in a foyer full of yawning celebrities in their nighties (Danny La Rue, Marianne Faithful) or pyjamas (the cast of a Broadway musical). The Sebel was the Tussaud's of Elizabeth Bay, with mobile waxworks.

Then I moved north and worked at 2UE, with such distinguished alumni as John Laws, Alan Jones and Stan Zemanik. After my late shift I'd go to Signatures to wind down, as would visiting rockers fatigued from filling a stadium. They'd drift in from the legendary Terry's Bar, hidden behind Reception and by midnight the restaurant was getting interesting. Addicted to celebs Brett Whitely, wearing his little flowerpot hat, was already ensconced in the hope of getting into conversation with someone famous.

One night Brett and I were mumbling to each other when we found ourselves waved at by a large blond lady sitting alone across the room. When she invited us to join her Brett was enraptured to discover that she was Mary, previously of 'Peter, Paul and' fame. Her former self a shadow of this post-trio Mary, she was a very hearty, funny lady. Lots of laughs.

Not so funny was Sir Robert Helpmann who, prior to Nureyev's defection, had been Dame Margot Fonteyn's favourite partner. Bobby would sit alone in his window seat staring sadly into the night. And, although he hadn't pas-de-deu'd for decades, wearing full stage make-up.

One night he had exciting news. 'I've got an acting part in a film in New Zealand.' 'Good money?' 'A thousand!' 'A day?' 'A week'. A great dancer on the dole. Whereas Nureyev died worth hundreds of million.

Long before Hugh Jackman would immortalise the Boy from Oz I spent hours talking – no, listening – to Peter Allen – who was on his way back to the US to be 'between the moon and New York City'. Peter was about to premiere his new musical on Legs Diamond and insisted I sit there for hours as he gave me a preview. Of the entire show. From the overture to final curtain. Peter sang all the parts for all the songs while conducting an imaginary orchestra, confident he'd be filling his mantelpiece with Emmys. For his words, his music, his starring role. Sadly the show was a flop. One of the only failures he suffered, if you exclude a surreal marriage to Lisa Minnelli.

Sometimes I didn't know who I was talking to. Had a great yarn about all sorts of non-musical things with a highly intelligent bloke from a rock-band I hadn't heard of. Dire Something. Told my daughters. Dad!!! You idiot!!! That was Dire Straits!! That was Mark Knopfler!!

Signatures, also the first place I met marvellous Magda Szubanski, is long gone. Now The Sebel's just condos. Should have been protected by a Green Ban or the National Trust. While fully occupied.

Thought versus Sport

I am opposed to sport on many grounds. Also on fields, ovals, courts and arenas. As the Olympic Games invariably demonstrate sport leads to hamstring injuries, concussion, pulled muscles, noxious nationalism, drug scandals, emotional problems, wrecked rooms and poor behaviour on aircraft. Hence my ongoing efforts to stamp it out. Sport is almost as dangerous as religion.

Decades ago I helped the great Melbourne journalist Keith Dunstan launch his Anti-Football League and, every year, we'd ritualistically destroy one of the VFL's silly inflated bladders – called as I recall Denzil Dons. Right there in the middle of the MCG. By blowing it up or having an elephant stomp on it.

When this brave campaign failed to gain universal support, I moved to Sydney and tried a different tactic. Disturbed by the violence in Rugby – all those lumbering brutes fighting over a ball – I recommended giving each team member a ball of his own to play with. Problem solved. Sadly officials refused to listen,

Time for a different tack. I announced the RSPCB. Yes, the Royal Society for the Prevention of Cruelty to Balls. From soccer to ping-pong to golf to billiards, poor harmless hapless innocent little balls are kicked, whacked, belted and thumped with boots, bats and clubs. Just as bad as taking baseball bats to Canadian seal pups.

But once again, disappointing results. I've yet to recruit enough members for a cricket team.

So this is it. My final effort. If people demand competition, let it be of brain rather than brawn. Announcing my new Olympic Games – to carry the torch of intelligence. Let Thought replace Sport! Mind over

Muscle! Tossing ideas instead of javelins! If you must have conflict let it be of Ideas! Let's putt arguments instead of shotting puts! Discussions not discus!

Instead of the sprint, a race to write a short story. Or mirror the marathon by tackling something a little longer, like Proust's A la recherché du temps perdu. Feats of strength replaced by feats of memory – as Mensa members fight to recall the entire text of the Bible or Koran, thus encouraging religious tolerance.

Fans of the high jump will thrill instead to tests for high IQ. Lots of quizzes of course – a form of sport – provided by *Millionaire Hot Seat*, *Hard Quiz* and *Mastermind*.

Book reading instead of bike riding or boat rowing. Hear the crowds cheer as fast-readers shave seconds off a chapter. And that's before we add other artistic pursuits to the program. Portraiture! Landscape painting! Olympic opera! Choral singing! Duets instead of mixed doubles! Ballet instead of gymnastics, though they obviously overlap.

As you might have noticed there is a shortage of intelligence in the community – as seen in anti-vaxx demonstrations and in the cognitively challenged dolts we elect to our parliaments and corporate boards. Now is the time to find new heroes – and candidates – in the ranks of the thoughtful, the literate. I'm confident of bipartisan support from One Nation and the Nats.

Thought instead of Sport. And think about this. My Mind Games, the Olympics of the Intellect, will not bankrupt the host city by demanding costly new buildings and arenas. They can be held at Oxford, the ANU, Harvard, UNSW, Cambridge. Training facilities? TAFE, plus our state schools and local public libraries.

Let the games begin. I see my old mate Barry Jones carrying the torch and lighting the cauldron.

Detectives

True story. Princess Di confided to me her mother-in-law's favourite TV show. We're talking the early 80s – long before Peter Morgan's *The Crown*. Not that one imagines that Royal soap's too popular at the Palace. You'd never guess. According to Di HM was addicted to an American crime series starring Telly Savalas as the bald, lollipop-licking *Kojak*. Di preferred *Dynasty*. Doesn't everyone have a favourite detective? With countless thousands in contention. Britain has the megastar in Sherlock Holmes, Agatha Christie gave us Hercule Poirot, Tuppence Beresford and Miss Marple. Recent additions are dominated by Denmark and its neighbours in the Scandi-noir cluster.

But, as in most things, America dominates – Los Angeles in particular – ranging from the army of Raymond Chandlerian private eyes and dicks to the LAPD's amazingly named Hieronymus Bosch.

Australia has a few indigenous sleuths. In the 1960s Arthur Upfield's devised a detective with the equally improbable name of Napoleon Bonaparte. Now we've *Mystery Road*'s taciturn Jay Swan who can go for an entire series without changing expression.

Detectives come in every ethnicity. Apart from Christie's Belgian fop there was the offensively stereotypical Chinese Charlie Chan and the Russian Arkady Renko by America's Martin Cruz Smith.

Many detectives have physical or mental issues. America's *Monk* and *The Bridge*'s Saga Noren are just two on the spectrum. J.K. Rowling's Cormoran Strike has one leg. Australia's Emma Viskic devised a deaf detective in Caleb Zelic – and I've found a few blind private eyes. Apart from such defective detectives there's a dog detective – Rex – a kangaroo detective – Skippy – a cyborg called Inspector Gadget. And a couple of investigators are given the unfair advantage of supernatural powers.

In the 1930s Dashiell Hammett gave us a thin detective played by William Powell and more recently we've had an obesity crisis of fatties. Robby Coltrane fleshed out *Cracker*, Richard Griffiths weighed in as *Pie-in-the-Sky*'s Henry Crabbe – both outweighed by the morbidly obese Nero Wolfe from the appropriately named Rex Stout. And lets honour Hector Crawford for casting the corpulent comedian Lucky Grills as heavyweight Detective Seargent Bluey Hills.

(Like *Law and Order*'s Dick Wolf our Hector was a Henry Ford of detectives, mass-producing them on a televisual assembly line. Add them up from *Homicide* to *Matlock* and my old mate Hec's body count exceeded *Midsummer Murders*'). Detectives often come as double-acts. Playing homage to Sherlock Holmes and his amanuensis Watson we've had that man of medical mystery Gregory House with his friend Wilson. Poroit pairs with the hapless Hastings. Monk with sidekick Sharona.

Aristocratic detectives? Lord Peter Wimsey (assisted by his butler) and Lady Lara Croft. Lower classmates? The rumpled Columbo with his half-smoked cigar and most of the cast of *Hill Street Blues*.

Women detectives abound – not just Agatha Christies'. Jessica Fletcher, Nancy Drew, Olivia Benson, Cagney and Lacey, Dana Scully, Lisbeth Salander, Charlie's Angels, Jane Tennison, Maddie Hayes, Clarice Starling. Louise Milligan. Crime is an equal opportunity industry.

Trends. DNA has been a part of detection for decades, taking over from fingerprints. Think NCIS series with their newfangled forensics. It's only a matter of time until we hand detection over to algorithms. As in Spielberg's *AI*, a project he took over from Kubrick. Or his Minority Report that solves murders before they occur. Here they come – Holmes and Watsons rendered robotic.

As Sargent Estahaus warned in *Hill Street*, 'be careful out there'.

Dogs in Heaven

Today's sermon sets out to answer that most profound of theological questions 'do dogs go to Heaven?'.

During the pandemic the price of puppies soared as people sought the solace of animal companions. Dogs previously doomed to be euthanized are now welcomed into family homes. Even surplus greyhounds.

So will pooches make it into Paradise? According to Pope Francis the answer is yes. The Holy Father put it in writing to a young boy whose dog had died – confirming Vatican issues visas to pets. Apparently not all Cardinals agree but the boss is, as we know, infallible.

But does it apply only to dogs that are pets? What about working dogs? Dingoes? Wild dogs? Retired sniffer dogs? Obviously seeing-eye dogs, though not categorised as pets, have strong arguments in their favour. The devil's in the detail and we await clarification from Rome.

As we know humanity is divided into dog people and cat people. So what about pet cats? After 9 lives do they have an everlasting 10th? Chasing pet mice? What about goldfish? Lizards? Tortoises? Canaries? Budgies? Horses? I'm sure lots of Middle-Easterners have pet camels. Though not well regarded in Genesis, some people have pet snakes. I've had a pet kangaroo that followed me everywhere. Even into the shower. He grew up hopping around the studio at 2UE. And once peed on Paul Keating's Zegna suit. What rapturous reunions wait! What a zoo it will be!

My ruminations are a response to a letter from a reader incensed by a column doubting life after death, even for humans. But I gladly concede that all life-forms can look forward to continuing existence post-mortem in a sort of Carl Sagan-ish pantheism. As Carl reminded us, we are all made of 'star stuff' and our atoms will be recycled. But our consciousness? Egomaniacal surely.

And are all humans entitled to go to Heaven? Neanderthals and other related species? All the hominoids that preceded our god-like status? Java Man? Flores Man. The Neanderthals? If it depends on the kindling of a soul, when did evolution provide one?

Given 100,000,000,000 clearly defined humans have already lived and died it must be getting overcrowded up there, so you'd assume there are policies in place. To paraphrase our greatest political deity John Winston Howard 'we will decide who comes and the circumstances by which they come'.

Judaism is iffy on the existence of an afterlife. The Jehovah' Witnesses limit the entire intake to a miserable 144,000. The Vatican is more generous. Even non-Christians may be accepted, but only after a period in Christianity's Purgatory, aka Christmas Island. Hinduism opts for recycling; Islam believe the dead are in an intermediary state until 'the great resurrection'.

Death? I believe that what happens after your death is an endless nothingness. If wrong I shall report back, provided Heaven has Wi-Fi

Talking of science – wealthy people have been having their diseased cadavers deep-frozen in the hope of more personal resurrections. And other billionaires are wont to have their consciousness cyrovac'd – in the form of their minds being downloaded. Clearly we cannot face the future without the lingering presence of our Elon Musks.

I don't recall Jesus having a pet dog. If so Da Vinci neglected to depict it in the Last Supper, though he may have been out of sight under the table being surreptitiously fed scraps. After all, every US President had a 'first dog'. Except Trump.

Dogs yes. Donald no.

Lan Choo Coupons

Long ago, when we were both young and full of promise, Paul Hogan and I were amused by the fact that both us had, at the same time, discovered the nostalgic joys and satirical possibilities of our mums' kitchen drawer. He in a TV sketch, me in a column.

Both of us remembered all the bits 'n bobs within, the archaeological layers of domestic detritus revealed by a good rummage. There were thick 'n thin rubber bands of all sizes, pieces of salvaged string, a few postage stamps, old receipts and a some recipes cut from the *Woman's Weekly*, broken pencils and dry Biro's… and most precious of all, some carefully hoarded Lan Choo coupons – the ends of packets of a popular tea brand.

Lan Choo coupons were the first loyalty program. Long before Qantas' irremediably irritating and irredeemable Frequent Flyer Points – in that once-upon-a-time time when frequent flying was not merely feasible but legal – Lan Choo coupons were Frequent Drinker Points, a marketing strategy aimed at challenging the dominance of other brands. Mums stored them in the drawer in the hope of redeeming them for tea towels.

At that pre-decimal time the official Australian currency was LSD, pounds, shillings and pence. There was even a sterling version of the $ sign, a quid symbol long since vanished, on your typewriter keyboard. But the Lan Choo coupon had much the same financial heft as the Bitcoin today. You could face the future secure in the knowledge that you'd always have an assured supply of tea towels.

Could those relying on the Yen, the Yuan, the Zloty, the Deutschmark, the Dinar, the Dong, the Peso, the Rouble, the Baht and the Shekel say as much? Here was a currency you could trust not to be damaged by recession or devalued by inflation or hyperinflation. Not even gold's as good. If only the Lan Choo was still with us, mentioned by Alan Kohler on the *ABC News* along with the US $, the stock market results and the oil price.

And though I'm not into conspiracy theories other than the ones I make up, why wasn't the unsung hero who coined the Coupon given the Nobel Prize in Economics? Clearly someone in Oslo cooked the books.

I cannot bring myself to have faith in the new-fangled Euro. If only the ATM at the office dished out Lan Choo coupons I could face the uncertain post-Covid future.

And here's the odd thing. Clearly our mums treasured the coupons more than the fabrics they could receive on redemption. Neither Paul nor me could remember any Lan Choos actually being cashed in. They were simply clipped and collected and kept in the drawer among the rubber bands and dry Biros, perhaps to be willed to the next generation. I suspect that somewhere there's a huge hangar full of tea towels waiting for a home, soon to be joined by vast amounts of unloved, unwanted AstraZeneca.

May I suggest a compromise? Lan Choo Credit and/or Debit cards. Not silver like Amex. Green, like the coupons. And maintaining the Frequent Drinking principle if only to reduce our caffeine consumption. And to keep pace with the current crisis redeemable for face masks rather than tea towels.

Stop the press. I've just snuck into Woolies to discover that Lan Choo is still on the shelves, that it's a Bushells' brand, in the traditional loose-leaf form. Have a cuppa while I arrange a summit meeting with Bushells and report back.

Body Parts

We tend to take ourselves for granted. But pandemics require a rethink. Suddenly our plumbing arrangements become problematic requiring endless tests and puncture marks. In my case I'm way out of warranty and spare parts are no longer available.

My regular maintenance requires quite a few batteries, one whopper implanted to keep a pacemaker ticking over – and some little rechargeables for hearing aids. Amongst other prosthetics – two artificial hips and a few pairs of specs. Over the years various organs have been surgically removed and their functions replaced by pills. My continued existence is a credit to a score of medical professionals.

But let's talk about you. You are approximately 99% comprised of six elements – oxygen, hydrogen, nitrogen, carbon, calcium and phosphorous. All put together for reproductive purposes. Let's start with the ears. Two oddly shaped orifices, one on each side, for the purposes of hearing, plus lobes for earrings. Other things come in twos too – include two eyes for looking, two cheeks for noshing and two nostrils for breathing, sneezing and smelling. Some also use the nostrils for cocaine sniffing. These are aligned within just one nose, also designed to prop your sunnies.

But only one mouth. Talk about a busy day at the orifice. We make so many demands on the poor mouth. For our eating, drinking, burping, sucking, spitting and regurgitating. And vocalising! Talking is the predominant noise, punctuated by some yelling and occasional bursts of song. The mouth also produced saliva and contains a tongue and tastebuds – plus teeth for mastication and dental cavities. I think that's got it covered.

O, forgot that ears are also useful for keeping your specs in place.

This being a family magazine I'm reluctant to go below the waist, but it has to be admitted that what the mouth ingests a few miles of intestines and a stomach process for nutrition prior to heading deep south for the bowels, which we can take as read. Ditto the naughty bits – the simple and silly-looking male genitalia and the more discreet female counterpart. We'll skip all this as it involves sex, which, in the absence of birth control rightly frowned upon by the Vatican, leads to babies. But I suppose I must admit to the existence of breasts, primarily designed for lactation rather than lust.

I think that God (or Evolution – that depends on you) made a serious mistake with sex, the source of some brief amusement but enormous trouble. I would have opted for the approach of sexless single cellular reproduction. The amoeba has much to teach us, including a form of celibacy (cellibacy?) that would have saved us so much unnecessary stress.

Have I left out anything? Sensory perceptions? Perhaps some details on the lungs, liver, kidneys, veins, arteries, glands, muscles, spleens, spinal cords, and thyroids. We're quite complicated really. Perhaps overcomplicated – which leads to things going wrong? And I forgot skin, our version of leather upholstery. And what about hair? Not enough of it to keep you warm, and in such unlikely places and tufts. Requires a lot of combing and cutting. And clipping and shaving. Never quite seeing the point of hair, I welcomed baldness. So forget follicles – and teeth are over-rated. Instead of having a gobful of different ones we'd be better off with two ceramic arcs. Less nooks and crannies for decay. Good morning.

Catching Covid

HEALTH WARNING: this column contains data on Delta you may choose to ignore.

I speak for every patriotic Australian in praising the real US President for his leadership during the pandemic. We believed him when he dismissed Covid as a bad cold and echoed his belief that it would disappear like 'a miracle'. Not because of some yet-to-be invented vaccination but because of the power of prayer. And/or by following his instructions in drinking detergent. We cheerfully blew Trumpian raspberries at that quack Anthony Fauci – while scorning all pandemical medical advice from local stooge Norman Swan. Even when the US death toll topped 700,000, the World's 5,000,000 and Australia's 1,400 we did not fear walking through the valley of death because Trump, 'the chosen one', was with us. We preferred Presidential optimism to fake vaccines. Plus the prayers of his favourite Pentecostals – taking particular comfort from The President's 'personal spiritual advisor' Paula White – and that most energetic of evangelists Kenneth Copeland who, memorably, 'banished Covid to hell' by simply laughing at it. And I quote 'HA HA HA HA!!!'

But me of little faith began to think that perhaps, just perhaps, a jab or two might, just might help. That perhaps, just perhaps, anti-vaxxers were nuts. Not fussing over Pfizer, we were happy to take anything available. Even the accursed Astra-Zeneca, made unpopular by the same Federal Government that failed utterly to provide adequate supplies of Pfizer.

So while still sending donations to Paula, Kenneth and Hillsong, Patrice and I got double-vaccinated. Only to become two of the unfortunate few who still got Covid. I disappeared from my radio program for weeks while quarantined on the farm, effectively home-hospitalised. I reveal this now we've fully recovered (thanks to AZ the symptoms were mild) and because we want to thank NSW Health for their remarkable efforts.

First a nurse made a five hour round trip from Newcastle to explain how to use various devices that would be monitored remotely on a daily basis. Friendly and very professional nurses would phone every day on the dot, ask for our temperatures, pulse rate, oxygenation levels etc. Blessings upon you Kylie, Barbara and Rhianna. And thanks to the local policeman who'd drive to the farm, don the full Covid cossie, to make sure we were behaving. Until finally, NSW Health gave us a clean bill of health.

Consider that through this period the crisis was escalating and the caseload soaring – from the low hundreds into the thousands every day. NSW Health, under an impossible workload, managed countless cases like ours. Aided by their professionalism NSW Health got us through it.

A brilliant effort from a much-maligned bureaucracy. We sing their praises and thank them.

Trumpian nonsense still abounds, as do inane, insane and deadly dangerous demos that demonstrate only terminal stupidity. Local Trumpians like Clive Palmer buy quantities of Donald's fake-cure hydroxychloroquine – while Federal politicians market misinformation on an industrial scale via social media, adding to the menu such poisonous nonsense as a drug designed for horses. Even the riots are Trumpian, reminiscent of the storming of the Capitol. And the first responders – the doctors and nurses in our hospitals and the people at NSW Health – face abuse.

Yes, many conspiracy theorists die from their own delusions – particularly in the Trump-Republican states of the US. Still denying Covid on their deathbeds.

Meanwhile the treasonous Trump plots to run again in 2024... and might very well win. Talk about miracles.

Audio Books

For almost 40 years I've been commuting between Sydney and the bush. Mostly nocturnal. A round trip of 600 kms, a grand total nudging 1,000,000, in terms of time I'm at the wheel for stretches of 4 to 5 hours, depending on the vagaries of traffic. The scenery is literally all too familiar and holds no mystery – except for the locations of new potholes. My only real distractions have been encounters with drugged or deranged truck drivers whose aggression has, like *Duel* (the first and best of Spielberg's movies) been near fatal on a dozen occasions. Plus collisions with kamikaze kangaroos leaping through the windscreen at 3am.

To fill the time I've listened to audiobooks – thousands upon thousands of old-style cassettes evolving into CDs and, currently, download via Bluetooth. I gave up on radio early – the signals come and go – and stopped listening to music. Anything too lyrical worked like a lullaby and made me dangerously sleepy. Too exciting (remember Ride of the Valkyries in *Apocalypse Now*?) and I'd accelerate into expensive trouble with the constabulary. Augmented by the dreaded points system.

So an old grain silo converted into a library holds not only 10,000 books but also decades of audiobooks. Their readers, and the authors, have been my companions for almost 1,000,000 kms. Most of the titles I've forgotten – but others are fresh in the memory and are sometimes revisited. Kenneth Branagh's sublime read of *Pepys' Diaries* for example, and a long-lost cassette of Lauren Bacall reading Dorothy Parker. Lots of CDs read by John le Carre – not only his own on George Smiley et al but books written by others. Le Carre reads wonderfully, as scholarly with accents as Henry Higgins. And sometimes I go for crime fiction with local favourite Emma Viskic or David Suchet reading – channelling – Poirot.

An audio book, at its best, is an art form of its own. Not good or better than the book itself (what Dame Edna used to call the choice of 'limp' or 'stiff') but different and distinct, an effortless variation on reading. I reckon Pepys would be enthralled by Branagh and can hear Porter laughing at the throaty Bacall. Highly recommended – Douglas Adams reading his wildly imaginative misadventures of Arthur Dent.

I avoid one form of audiobook – the studio dramatization with half a dozen actors and sound effects. Usually an unhappy hybrid.

But one problem remains with the solo read. The need to be, in effect, half a dozen actors providing the voice for the hero, the villains, the extras. Only a few thespians have sufficiently flexible throats – even for characters of their own genders. Crunch time is when a male reader has to speak for a female – often resulting in embarrassing falsettos – or vice versa when a woman tried to lower her voice a few octaves for a bloke. On balance I prefer the reader to simply read all 'the parts' in his or her own voice, allowing timing, context and the listener to do the rest.

You can tell that audiobooks are a growing phenomenon when the like of Amazon muscle in – and not just for we road-readers like me. As sight dims with the elderly – making television problematic – it's great to have a book read to you.

And NOT by the author. Le Carre aside most authors may write like angels but can't read to save themselves. Now, back to the new Donna Leon.

NDE

Many claim to have had an NDE, a 'near death experience'. On briefly karking it they report being welcomed to another realm by a shimmering figure or some-such. All very lyrical and reassuring. However, two of my friends were technically dead for a time – the ABC's Robyn Williams and ACP's Kerry Packer. Neither returned with glad tidings confirming an afterlife though Kerry found his glimpse of Beyond liberating. 'There's no one there to greet you. There's no one there to judge you. So you can do what you effing well like.'

I've also knocked on death's door and heard it creaking open – following a couple of botched surgical procedures. And then there was the time I almost died laughing. Not metaphorically, literally. And the figure I saw was not angelic but a drunken French postman.

My NDE was at the Dendy Cinema in Brighton around 60 years ago. I was watching the first feature directed by Jacque Tati in 1949, a few years before his masterpiece *Mr. Hulot's Holiday*. *Jour de Fete* was set in the rural village of Saint-Severe-sur-Indre with the villagers providing most of the cast. It tells of the blunderings of the postman – played by Tati – on the big day the carousel starts spinning in the town square, along with a few tatty sideshows and a tent cinema. And the damned film damn near killed me.

The sight gag that almost did me in involved the postie, inebriated during the festivities, completing his round on a rickety bicycle that also seemed inebriated. Tati parks the thing beside a fence and, when attempting to remount. swings a ludicrously long leg over both bike and fence. Despite his persistent efforts this made it impossible to pedal. I was convulsed. Nothing in Chaplin or Keaton had had the same effect.

Choking for air, my heart wildly palpitating I felt myself slipping from the seat onto the floor among the lolly wrappings – and started to lose consciousness. I knew that, yes, I was laughing myself to death. There are worse ways to go (as I'd discover later in a long life) but then, dying in the Dendy, I was dimly aware of the irony.

You have been warned. I saw the film in black and white. Subsequently restored by Tati's daughter in the experimental colour system used in the filming but deemed a failure. This polychrome version is currently proffered on SBS World Cinema. I've found the courage to download it but not the courage to watch it. Having narrowly survived in my youth – apparently my companions saved me without the need for an ambulance – I lack the bravery to tempt fate and fatality by meeting Tati's Francois a second time. The Grim Reaper in the guise of a French postman.

Don't mention the War. Tati's film is set in a bucolic, sentimentalised France just after the defeat of the Nazis. Which recalls the Monty Python sketch about the joke that killed Germans. Deemed the funniest joke ever told, it was amplified and broadcast at the Hun by brave British troops wearing earplugs. On the receiving end of this weaponised wit the Nazis would stand, stiffen and topple like ninepins. One hopes that this joke is now under lock and key and, like poison gas and other chemical weapons banned by the Geneva Convention.

Being given what Spike Milligan's Bluebottle called 'the dreaded deadings' via laughter is all most amusing. Unless you've had my experience at the dreaded Dendy.

Arthur Hodges

I'm twelve. Attending school in a pre-gentrified working class Richmond – at the Yarra Park State School, a prepubescent version of the Blackboard Jungle. Its playground – that term a total misnomer – is a cruel place, where I'm 'picked on' as a middle-class blow in. Until the arrival of the wildly eccentric Adrian Rawlins, these days memorialised by a statue in Fitzroy. I join in picking on him. But Adrian's another story

I'm a member of a local Scout troop that meets in the basement of a bluestone Anglican church. Until I'm expelled for setting the scoutmaster's desk on fire. But that too is another story.

One night my friend Arthur Hodges and I decide to wag the broomstick warriors and go to Hoyts Cinema, a drafty barn on Bridge Street next to the Richmond Town Hall. I've many memories of the place, including local bikies riding up and down the central aisle in deafening approval of Marlon Brando's *The Wild One*. Hoyts Cinema was that sort of cinema.

Arthur and I have snuck off in our scouts' uniforms to see a double-bill of horror movies. Seventy years on I'm not entirely sure what they were. Almost certainly a *Frankenstein* with Boris Karloff and a *Dracula* with Bela Lugosi, the evening complete with a Cinesound Newsreel, Val Morgan slides, movie trailers and, for light relief amongst the horrors, a cartoon. We sit about half way down and watch the horror show. Or rather, I watch it. Petrified by the prospect of vampires and monsters Arthur sits beside me curled in the foetal position, his Scout hat over his face. All he sees that night is the inside of his hat.

'What's happening? What's happening now?' asks a trembling voice, muffled by the Baden Powell headgear. And I attempt a running commentary. 'There's a lot of lightning and stuff and the creature is starting to twitch!!' 'Now it's sitting up and breaking the leather straps!' Or 'the vampire is sinking his teeth into her throat and starting to suck her blood'. To which Arthur responds with piteous moans as he clamps his hat more firmly on face, as though it were Ned Kelly's armour or a medieval knight's protective crash helmet.

You will be familiar with the terms 'a cheap drunk' – someone who gets inebriated on even the smell of alcohol. My friend Arthur was a 'two-pot screamer', someone who starts screaming at the very thought of disturbing imagery, no matter how tamely evoked on the screen. He didn't need to see Boris lumbering around with bolts in his neck – or Bela's protruding fangs. To even glimpse the goings-on might have caused cardiac arrest.

I don't think he ever saw – really saw – a horror film. Not *The Beast With Five Fingers* when a hand crudely amputated from the wrist of a concert pianist takes on a life of its own and crawls around like a fleshy crab seeking victims to strangle. Or Lon Chaney sprouting facial hair as he transmogrifies in the *Wolf Man*, before being euthanized by a silver bullet. He never saw Dracula desperately trying to climb into his coffin to escape the first shaft of sunlight. Or Frankenstein's melancholy monster being driven into the swamp by angry villagers brandishing burning torches.

These days Dr. Frankenstein's dated. Ditto Dracula and the Wolfman. Now we have Covid and its variants to fear – and the return of that variant on the *Addams Family*, Donald and the Family Trump. Or local horrors like Michaelia Cash in full banshee mode, or a Barnaby Joyce press conference.

So Arthur, if you're still around keep the hat on your face. We dwell in even spookier times.

2022

Memory

Many years ago – more than I can actually remember – the late Bob Ellis and I conducted a memory experiment. With fellow writer Annie Gillison we decided to choose a year, pretty much at random, and see what we could recall about it. No Googling then, no Wikipedia. Just the mind's eye.

We began by going solo. Writing personal lists without discussion. Log ones. But then things slowed down and pretty much petered out. Not only the political and the cultural but the personal. Then we opened things up and the strangest thing happened or began to. By bouncing off each other memories began to trickle – and flood. Not that our lives had much intersected – I hardly knew Ann while Bob and I, at that stage in our lives, weren't close. Yet we experienced an unstoppable, exhilarating process. Together we were more than the sum of our parts.

Before his death Bob I and talked out the experiment – and the conviction we had at the time that – given the right stimulus almost everything that ever happens to us can be recalled. At some point Bob had read of fine needles being pushed into a brain and apparently triggering the same phenomenon as our séance. Given a jiggle the synapses start firing and out of the depths of the subconscious. Could it be that we remember everything? That it's all stored in the attic or basement?

This ancient scribe has never been persuaded by 'repressed memory'. I've got countless memories I'd like to repress but no luck. Could it be that rather than repressing or 'pressing the delete' these damned brains of ours are hoarders? Between our ears we house 100,000,000,000 neurons, and that's before you factor in those pesky synapses. (If you don't believe me ask Google, our collective memory). That many neurons is often compared with the number of stars in our Galaxy – but that's an overstatement. The Milk Way has three times the stars. But 86,000,000,000 remains astronomical.

Intelligent life in Outer Space? Remember Eric Idle's whimsical request for evidence of intelligent life on Earth. Evidence for stupidity abounds – notable on our politicians and the people who vote for them. But our individual noggins are, quite clearly, super-computational. On the one had we can't remember where we left our car keys. On the other we came up with the Theory of Relativity.

Not all neurons are born equal. Trying to measure IQ, The common fruit fly has 2,500 that count. The bee? 170,000. The common house mouse has 14,000,000. The budgie has 146,00,000. The elephant, with its legendary memory, 6,775,000,000. Onward ever upward.

But enough. Like those blokes in Monty Python, thinking makes my brain hurt.

Back to my original issue. Do we remember everything? Or rather, can we if we ask the brain the right questions? I haven't the foggiest – and the experts seem to disagree. Perhaps even our billions of neurons need their rest and relaxation and chuck lots of memories out. Like the stuff we leave on the footpath for council collection. It's also fascinating that we remember stuff that didn't actually happen – like dreams and songs. Tunes and lyrics. People collect these enormous song lists and keep them on their iPhones or similar thingo's with, yes, huge memories. But I remember vast numbers of songs I didn't like in the first place.

Where the hell are my car keys?

Republic

As we approached 2000 many hoped we'd finally deal with 'the three R's' – Reconciliation, Refugees and the Republic. In 2022 they still represent our greatest failures.

R number one: Reconciliation is rarely mentioned. The term has vanished from our national vocabulary. The best, most noble attempt to deal with that greatest shame, to heal that deepest wound, the treatment of the indigenous people over the last 200 years, has been effectively rejected. The Uluru Statement –'the Message from the Heart' – has been either ignored or attacked. Political ill-will and cowardice continues to rule the day, the decades, the centuries.

R number two: Refugees. The White Australia Policy lives on. The ongoing horror story of their illegal mistreatment adds to our international shame – except with those who admire and adopt its cruelties – as in recent times have the Conservative governments in the UK.

R number three: The Republic. Despite the wreckage that is the Windsor dynasty – culminating in Charles' 'honours for cash' scandal and the perversions of brother Andrew – we remain a monarchy. John Howard, who helped scuttle our last attempt at constitutional dignity, must be delighted.

Thus under the Australian Constitution we have only two prerequisites for our Head of State – following the British Act of Settlement (1701). Our King or Queen must not be a Catholic but must be a descendant of the Electress Sophia of Hanover. Are you proud and patriotic, dear reader, that we have so far met these conditions?

My friend and fellow Republican Barry Jones AC quotes Robert French, later Chief Justice of the High Court, writing in 2008. "The legal Head of State... can never be chosen by the people or their representatives, cannot be other than a member of the Anglican Church, can never be other than British and can never be an indigenous person". Happy with that? For this multicultural, pluralistic, independent and – one hopes – irreverent Australia?

Let us have a plebiscite on a Republic. Yes or No. Then a Constitutional referendum on the precise form it should have. Let us have a constitution that honours the First Australians – that even finds space to mention the existence of a Prime Minister or a cabinet. Or, for that matter, an Opposition. Believe it or not, the current one does not. Oops.

I share with Barry – who himself would make a fine President – an enthusiasm for the Irish model. As Barry points out the six Presidents since Valera have not challenged the Taoiseach and have behaved very 'Bill Deane-ishly'. All have been supported by one party – sometimes by all of them – and no one who ran for a second term was challenged. For the reassuring details read Barry's recent book *What Is To Be Done*.

Both major parties have been very silent on the Republican issue- and there's no denying polling shows declining support for change. But sadly there's declining support – and deepening doubt for anything 'political'. Surely we're overdue for a sane and serious discussion of our future? The very act of having it may energise our dilapidated democracy. On coming into being a Constitution for the 21st Century would deal with two of 'the three R's'. A good, albeit slow, start.

A plebiscite pretty please. Then onto a referendum on the nuts and bolts. And fear not – few want a model that would deliver a Trumpian president- or one with US style powers.

PS. Did you know that currently the Governor General is Chief of the Armed Forces? Neither did I.

Nuddy Pole

Of the minimalist puzzles in zen koans my favourite is 'imagine the sound of one hand clapping'. As that sound is a prelude to this column please do so now.

All hail minimalism. I recall with pleasure the minimalist approach to foreign policy mooted by an upstart Dutch political party. Any country annoyed by the Netherlands would ring a hotline and hear a recorded message. 'We surrender!'.

I also preferred the so-called 'minimalist approach' to a hypothetical Australian republic. Simply replace Governor General with President on all the Yarralumla stationery. Easy peasy,

A few weeks ago I chaired a discussion on the Australian Republican Movement's new model – controversially involving a form of direct election. It co-starred Peter FitzSimons (the red bandana-crowned king of the ARM), erstwhile Foreign Minister Bob Carr and constitutional expert Prof. Anne Twomey who at one point asked a mischievous question – 'Why have a head of state at all?'

This recalled the issue of the Australian flag which, as a lifetime member of the Ausflag committee, I've long wanted changed. At least getting rid of the Union Jack stuck in the top corner like a stamp on an envelope, directing any patriotic feelings to the letterbox at Buck Palace. Then another novel thought struck. Why have a flag at all?

Flags are very dangerous pieces of fabric. We are not content to fly them and salute them and lower them to half-mast on sad occasions. Countless millions have died fighting for the wretched bloodstained things. The flag has draped an infinite number of coffins. So let me run a radical idea up the pole and see if you salute it.

Beloved readers and fellow patriots – instead of fighting over a putative design for a flag (just as we squabble over a putative republic) let's be the one-and- only nation without one. No fatal fabric. No flag.

Behold the nuddy pole!

Designing a flag is and always was a martial art. Flags date back to Ancient Egypt – as a rallying point in military conflicts. From then to Hitler's contribution – the fluttering swastika – they've been associated with megadeath and madness. I suspect there was a 'stars and stripes' painted on the bomb dropped on Hiroshima – and in Trump's insurrection at the Capitol they filled the air along with MAGA chanting. And please note that Australia has a proud tradition of following the US flag into US battles. Korea, Vietnam, Iraq and Afghanistan. Many Australian conservatives seem more inspired by their flag than their own.

So imagine your sense of peaceful pride when you stand outside the United Nations Building on the East River and look up at that long row of flags representing said nations... only to see one nuddy pole. It might puzzle some but soon they'd get the elegant simplicity of the Adams' idea – for which he'd claim neither royalties nor reward.

Apart from the cost savings this ultimate and inspired piece of minimalism would mean that people everywhere would think of Australia whenever they saw a nuddy pole. Every time a soldier from any nation lowered a flag at sunset there we'd be. Nuddy poles. More valuable than Blue Poles.

There's also an audible aspect. Flagpoles have a rope for raising and lowering these terrible textiles. So by all means let us keep the rope on our nuddy flagpole. Because it brings us back to the zen koan. You will hear the sound of one rope slapping.

Risk Assessment

How will our time at the peak of the evolutionary Everest end? How will we fall from grace? How will our world end – with a bang or a whimper?

Today's epistle? Risk assessment of the fates that await. And let's face it. We have enough of those Damoclean swords dangling over our head for a full dinner service.

Top of my list – as its been for forty years sine my Commission for the Future first blew the whistle on the Greenhouse Effect – is what became known, via Global Warming and other aliases – as Climate Change. Thanks to denialists in government and the lobbying power of the fossils running the fossil fuel industry, we are victims of ever-greater droughts, floods, bushfires, tornadoes and mass extinctions. Climate deserves its own Doomsday Clock – and we're seconds from the midnight of our own mortality. Millions of us may die of its consequences – if not from starvation then Covid-accelerated disease.

The original Doomsday Clock concerned itself with nuclear Armageddon and, during the Cold War, we could hear the noise clockwork makes just before striking. Now, decades later, with troops massing on various borders and the nuclear stockpile, stacked with more than 13,000 nukes yearning to burst from the bellies of bombers, submarines or underground missile sites, the clock once more is making its ominous sound. Among the proud owners of nuclear WMDs – the USA, Russia, China, India, Pakistan, the UK, France and Israel. With more, including North Korea, beating their nuclear pectorals.

Pandemics aplenty: HIV-AIDS still wreaks havoc. Ditto outbreaks of Ebola and our current crop of Covids. Time for a Covid Clock? Will we reach herd immunity before we're herded into the abattoir?

Oh, and UFOs are making a comeback, as evidenced by the release of military-grade photographs by the Pentagon to a US Congressional Enquiry. Suddenly Spielberg's *Close Encounters* looks like a documentary. A *War of the Worlds* to add to the inventory? I'm old enough to remember the good old days of Flying Saucers that fellow sceptics were easily able to rationalise – to explaining them away as misidentification of natural phenomena or simply wafting weather balloons. Or the testimony of ratbags. Suddenly we're heading back to Roswell. Here come the X-Files.

And there are other threats from outer space. The Universe is forever playing cosmic billiards – everything from comets to black holes. You may have heard of the problem the dinosaurs had when an errant asteroid struck our planet just 66,000,000 years ago – causing climate change to wipe out the dominant dinosaurs and give humans our evolutionary advantage. To borrow a title from Netflix – 'don't look up'.

Have I missed anything? Yes. Political apocalypses (apocolyae?) abound. One by one nations deemed to be democracies have fallen to dictators, demagogues or tyrants. Duterte in the Philippines, Bolsanaro in Brazil, Putin in Russia and fascists in Poland and Hungary. Not to mention the prime example of the treasonable Trump in the US – a President who choreographed an insurrection. Seems the Republicans are poised to win in the midterms while the Donald preps for another presidential run. From the land of the free to another failed state.

Thank God it couldn't happen in Australia. No QAnon in high places. No corruption gnawing away at the body politic. No climate change denialism in our upper echelons. Just a Labor Party full of Chinese spies and Manchurian candidates. What's that old saying? 'What could possibly go wrong?'

Votes for Trees

As you may remember I campaigned for many years to get trees the vote. As with the crusade for Women's Suffrage it was a long and bitter struggle – finally succeeding when won that recent referendum. Now trees can be enrolled – and we're trying hard to get as many as possible signed up for the forthcoming Federal Election. Regarding the LNP as our enemy and hope to defeat this anti-tree government in key electorates. We will then join with the Greens and hope to hold the balance of power in a hung parliament.

I believe 16 year-old humans should get the vote but don't have the numbers. Nor did I win this argument in relation to arboreal citizens. Rings will have to be counted and only trees 21 years or older enrolled. A height limit has also been imposed to eliminate voting by shrubs, suckers and saplings.

We will be standing trees in key marginals – avoiding those like oaks and elms that may have dual citizenship issues. We're running Deciduous for the Reps, Evergreen for the Senate and expect solid support from tree huggers in inner city electorates and, yes, from tree-changers.

Trees being trees, many with thick branches, we've had some problems with branch-stacking. But membership is booming in logging areas, particularly in old-growth forests and near pulp mills.

Trees deserve to participate in our democracy. When not burnt down in their billions because of LNP denialism of climate change trees provide homes for koalas and places for birds to sit. And as I know from childhood nothing beats a tree for climbing. Forget those metallic gadgets in council playgrounds. When I was six a peppercorn was my best friend. Hence my role as an advocate for the world of the wooden.

Even dead trees are great contributors to civilisation. Their corpses provide timber from cradle to coffin, for homes and furniture including front and backbenches in parliaments. Plus, the wood for the official Commonwealth pencils that dangle from strings in our polling booths. No trees, no pencils, no elections. Ask Anthony Green.

I think that I shall never see a poem as lovely as a tree. Hence their popularity in the arts. No trees, no handles for paintbrushes, so no Namatjira or Nolan. You'd be left with the dribblers like that pillock Pollock.

Trees are, if you'll forgive the pun, treemendous. They store nasty carbon and help with photosynthesis – oxygenating the very air we breath. And how do we thank them? With chainsaw and axe. (The axe, with its treacherous wooden handle). We encourage their mass murder – arboreal genocide – via climate vandalism and ring-barking. By bull-dozing or chopping them down wherever they're deemed an obstacle to development. It's a wonder trees don't tear themselves out by the roots and march on us. Crushing us beneath their weight.

No indignity is too great. Behold the mountains of wood pulp, or the way we turn trees into chopsticks.

Vote 1 for Trees at the next election. Take your wooden pencil and fight to save trees that are doing their very best to save you. And while you're at it plant a few. Or do a Hawkie and plant a billion.

Let me leave you with this thought. Bismarck, that mightiest of Prussians, used to excuse himself from meetings to go outside and hug a tree. He insisted it was spiritually refreshing. Thus Otto was history's first recorded tree-hugger.

Bill Smith

Bill Smith. It's hard to think of a simpler name than that of my grandpa. The bloke that 'brought me up' from the age of 2 to 10, from 194I to 1951, in the absence of my mother. Sylvia, his youngest daughter, was thoroughly enjoying the war. Dad, the Rev. Charles Adams, was a chaplain in New Guinea and Sylvia Adams, nee Smith, had a job in 'The Rationing' that she enjoyed much more than her life in the manse as wife of a Congregational minister in the Victorian city of Maryborough. No time for a husband or for a young child. So she handed me over to Bill Smith and his wife Maud Rebecca.

Bill had an identical twin Fred. There's another simple name. Fred Smith. Inseparable their entire lives as everything from gold miners to farmers they now lived in twin houses, side by side, at 798 High Street, East Kew. They were horticulturalists, growing flowers on just four acres to sell at the Victoria Market. Poppies and violets were a speciality, along with white chrysanthemums (or 'chrissies') for Mothers Day.

Bill, Fred, Maud Rebecca and our farm are, of course, long gone. I named my first daughter Rebecca in memory of Grandma while the farm is remembered by a street name. The farm was sub-divided, the brothers cheated out of the money by a corrupt real estate dealer, and was soon filled with new houses. Now old themselves. Their address, Violet Grove.

Grandpa was the perfect grandpa. Gruff, gentle and kind. Though probably in his mid-forties he seemed ancient to me, as gnarled and wrinkled as an old tree. We had a huge horse called Blossom and Grandpa tilled the earth with an iron plough in the same way farmers had for a thousand years. Grandpa used to let me stand between his arms as he ploughed. 76 years later I remember the day she had to die. I can hear the shot. See the pool of blood where she fell. Relive the scene of that great body being carted off.

Every morning at breakfast Bill Smith would prop *The Age* up on a bottle of Maud's tommy sauce and read me bits. I recall a story about a famine in China. 'Poor buggers', he said. Bill was no bigot. It was from him that I had my first lessons in social justice. I also remember sitting with my grandparents listening to 'the wireless', our only electrical appliance. (I call my radio show 'the little wireless program' in its memory). And I can hear his resonant baritone voice singing to friends and family on Saturday nights – standing by the open fire belting out 'The Old Rugged Cross' or 'On The Road to Mandalay'. Grandpa also did a recitation about a 'green-eyed dragon with thirteen tails' that was deliciously scary.

Grandpa would let me wind his black-and-brass clock on the mantelpiece. Nothing made me prouder. He'd won it as cricket trophy and promised to leave it to me in his will. But somehow it went missing – and I miss it still.

I could, should, write a book about Bill Smith. About his decency, his dignity, his sad death. But I never got around to an autobiography, instead telling scraps of our story in columns written over many decades. Scraps like this one. Which explains why I spent my first 10 years on a farm, and my last 36.

Vale Bill Smith.

Hawke

This column on Bob Hawke begins with a joke and ends with a fistfight. First the joke.

PM: 'There are two dead bodies on the Hume Highway. One's a dead kangaroo and the other's a dead politician. What's the difference?' PA: 'I dunno.' PM: 'There are skid marks before the kangaroo.'

All the funnier coming from a Prime Minister. His joke began our collection published as *The Penguin Book of Australian Jokes*. It sold a million and got us through a drought. Thanks Bob.

So how did our relationship end in the scuffle in an Ansett lounge witnessed by a horrified Sir Arvi Parbo? Troy Bramston should have interviewed me for his bio on Bob – I know a hundred stories, few to his credit. So let me try and explain the trajectory.

I was a wholehearted supporter of Hawkie when he was plotting against Bill Hayden. Bob's principal co-conspirator was the diminutive and aptly named John Button. Bill had elicited a promise that during the brutal negotiations the two wouldn't talk to each other. So I was the go-between, holding two phones, one in each hand. "Bob says", "John says". In this dishonourable way we honoured the promise.

What changed my mind? It wasn't the affairs – of which I knew, many thanks to first person accounts. Or his habit of wandering around hotel rooms in the nuddy – as reported to me by an aghast Premier Kirner. Nothing sexual about it with Joan – who was happy she "wasn't his type". It was just another aspect of Bob's notorious narcissism.

I wrote satirical columns on the libidinous PM saying that the vertical squirter in Lake Burley Griffin was synchronised with his ejaculations. But later, it seemed to me, the bigger problem was another form of moisture: tears. You'll recall that Bob constantly wept – which many saw as commendable, evidence of a modern manliness and emotional honesty. Trouble is Bob agreed – that his tears were proof of his extraordinary empathy.

Except that it wasn't. As I'd writen at the time Bob's tears, which gushed like the Snowy Mountains Scheme, might ostensibly be for children in poverty or for the victims of Tiananmen but were actually shed for himself, tears celebrating his almost ecstatic empathy. I wrote then and say it again. Most of the time his tears were fraudulent, theatrical. Sometimes Bob shed them in very close proximity to me. Accompanied by a manly hug, after a stirring speech on something, he'd dampen my shirt.

Is this response clouded by my deep affection for my friend the long-suffering Hazel? Perhaps. A little. But evidence for its truth lays in Bob's enraged reaction. We became and remained enemies – as witnessed by Sir Arvi in the Ansett Lounge.

That enmity was intensified by my admiration for Paul Keating whose ascension to the throne Bob fought so bitterly. Even my friendship with Barry Jones was an issue. Absurdly Hawke despised Barry out of jealousy. I remember an argument at a film premiere I was hosting. Bob made it clear that he couldn't tolerate people talking of Barry as the ALP's great intellect. As if Barry's IQ could be compared with his own!! Bob so loved the limelight there was never enough to share. With Jones or with Keating or with anyone.

Yes, I concur with Troy and history that Hawke was a fine PM. One of the best. But I disagree that he was a fine man.

Elephant Man

Kerry Packer was so convinced of his ugliness he'd compare himself to Joseph Merrick, the Elephant Man.

Surviving childhood polio with a palsied cheek that few if any noticed, Kerry believed that political cartoonists did. During his darkest days, when forced to self-identify as 'the Goanna', cartoons of Packer loomed large on editorial pages and he'd stare bitterly at them.

In his gloomy Bellevue Hill mansion Kerry spent most of his time in a small study dominated by an open fire. It was flanked on the left by the largest TV then available and on the right by a cabinet containing a number of guns – cannons – big enough to launch cruise missiles. But in fact designed to kill elephants.

A huge pair of tusks suggested success in this endeavour whilst an elephant's foot had been repurposed to hold fire irons. I'd protest his monstrous and murderous hobby, making sombre jokes that this Elephant Man should deed-poll his name from Packer to Pachyderm.

It's hard to comprehend the thrill-killers, the pleasure that some humans, if that's the correct term, get from mowing down an animal. So that they can he photographed standing proudly over a corpse – killing not for food but in taxidermal triumphalism.

I have to cull on the farm and even shooting bunnies with a .22 is a sad business. But to shoot an elephant? That essentially harmless herbivore? That magnificent and highly intelligent proboscidean survivor of the Pliocene? Criminal.

We're sitting in the study when Kerry makes a confession. 'I've had a phone call from Idi Amin'. Idi being the continent's most brutal despot, veritably Africa's Pol Pot.

'Why am I not surprised?' was my reply. 'It was only a matter of time until you two found each other. But why the call?'

'He's invited me to Uganda to shoot elephants.' A long silence. 'What would that do to my reputation?' Another long silence. 'I don't know about your reputation Kerry,' I finally replied 'but it will fuck Idi's'.

So Kerry declined and I began a campaign to convert him from killer to conservationist. This started by explaining the existential threat to Africa's elephants, not just from his ilk but from ivory poachers. Plus the loss of habitat and the increasing enmity of farmers whose small crops were trampled by elephants' migratory paths.

After the Packerderm pondered matters somewhat simultaneously a small miracle and a big guilt trip occurred. Kerry announced he'd save the elephant! Given Australia's Kimberly was free of small farms and was on much the same latitude as the elephants' homelands he'd import a few dozen breeding pairs and let them loose!

I tried to explain why this noble thought was not a good idea. What if heffalumps, like so many introduced animals before them, took off? With few natural enemies we might see a variation on the theme that gave Australia rabbit plagues, the pestilence of prickly-pear, cane toad infestations, European carp rooting our rivers, half a billion feral pigs, brumbies and camels. Feral elephants for effs-sake? Lumbering up and down St. George's Terrace? Crushing cars? Treading on Perth's pedestrians?

Suddenly I imagined the panicked political response... with a boost in funding for CSIRO – so that Frank Fenner could try to update and upscale his myxo... for jumbos.

Kerry's enthusiasm to save the elephant deflated as quickly as... as a zeppelin shot with one of his elephant guns. And not long afterwards a Royal Commission was hunting him.

Exit the elephant, enter the Goanna.

Bottom's Up

The political proverb 'there's no such thing as a safe seat' has been born out by the election. Thus some new buttocks are to be found on the front benches. Ditto on benches back and cross on both the green of the Reps and the red of the Senate. So it is time for me to remind you of the significance of the gluteus maximus in our body politic, our geography, iconography and wild life.

As I've pointed out in the past if Italy looks like a leg and the UK a royal chess piece Australia resembles a vast bottom squatting in the southern hemisphere – hovering over the cold toilet seat of the Antarctic. With Perth and Sydney on the hips and Adelaide as the sphincter. I apologise to Tasmania for the image, which doesn't do much for the Apple Isle.

The theme of big bottoms is taken up by our coat of arms – which adorns all government documents and correspondence and, of course, in giant form, our Parliament House. Bottoms up to the shield flanked by kangaroo and emu.

Let's start on the left – physical not ideological. The kangaroo has a huge bottom. Indeed much of its physique is in its bum – or if you're pedantic, its haunches. The head is comparatively small, not suggestive of high intelligence. In that regard it's a fair representation of our political representatives, many of whom have such low IQs I've granted them membership of DENSA, my MENSA for the unintelligent. They are obsessed with sitting. On their seats, on parliamentary sittings. They aspire to pre-selection for the safest seats possible. Seats, seats, seats. For an MP a seat is a treat. Along with their Senatorial colleagues they could eat a seat, particularly one in Cabinet.

Now let's look to the right. Behold the Emu. Notoriously dim-witted this oversized chook also has a small head – and an even more disproportionate bum than the 'roo. Please forget its absurdly long legs and neck for a moment. The Emu is, in essence, a big bum upholstered in feathers.

Thus all our imagery converges on the bottom. The bum. The backside. The nether regions. The arse. Or if you prefer Latin (or is it Greek?) the gluteus maximus. More than most of our governments, state and federal, are bottom heavy. One Nation, for example, is full of fools who should get off their butts, eccentric bottom-feeders who give us the bum's steer on things like Covid and climate and should be given the bum's rush. We should fit our parliamentary benches with ejector seats like jet fighters so that when rejected at an election they can be sent flying, perhaps to crash land in the Press Gallery.

But back to coats of arms. The whopper on Parliament House Canberra is wholly appropriate. The choice of heraldic figures was inspired. Other nations have griffins and dragons while about a dozen have eagles with one or two heads. But our kangaroo and the giant chook are perfect, emphasising the gravitational attraction of power over the force of intellect. In that spirit we should have a trouser of arms, not a coat.

PS. The best thing that can be said about our heraldry – evoking bums, buttocks, backsides, posteriors, rumps and fundaments, is that it anticipated recent fashion trends. Whilst confessing to not having kept up with the Kardashians, I understand that, thanks to them, the titanic tush is trending.

Cooking

Julia Child has had many children. Since her pioneering efforts in televising French cooking 'foody' telly has been a recipe for success – now challenging crime as the most popular subject for TV shows. SBS has a channel dedicated to chefs while commercial networks groan beneath the weight of Masterchefs and their ilk. Hail examples from Margaret Fulton to Kylie Kwong via Bernard King, Maggie Beer and Poh Ling. And I played a role in launching the career of one of our first celebrity chefs in Peter Russell-Clarke – but that as they say is another story.

To begin at the beginning. Julia Child (1912-2004) claims to have kicked off the industry in 1962 at WGBH in Boston quickly gaining national fame. Currently being portrayed by Sarah Lancashire (in *Julia* on Fox) she's previously been performed by Jean Stapleton, Meryl Streep and, in drag, by John Candy and Dan Ackroyd.

However, Child was not the first. Julia was preceded by Jean – right here in Australia. Jean Bowring had a cooking show at Channel 7 in Melbourne from 1957 to 1960. I know because it was my very first job in television, then just one year old. Screens were tiny and fuzzily black-and-white and telly was such a novelty that people still watched it in shop windows. The only non-American or non-British show on the ABC or commercial channels was the News, largely read out from the daily papers. Oh, Channel 7 did have a show called *The Hit Parade* where a few locals mimed to American records.

Paid just 5 quid a week and dossing in a single room a few miles away, I depended on Jean's TV leftovers to augment my meagre diet. At the end of each half hour program (previously just 15 minutes) there'd be a race between us – me, the camera crew, the floor manager and the boom swinger – for the crumbs from Jean's table. For the food on the set and flip-stands.

In those pre-digital days the 'tricks of the trade' were primitive. For example, filmmakers filled ice-cream cones with mashed-potato for their actors to lick – because the real thing quickly melted under the lights. And when dancing in the rain it was common to add milk to the mixture to make the downpour more visible. We should have remembered such legerdemain on the famous occasion of Jean Bowring's multi-layer sponge cake.

As Julia Child would learn it was essential for a TV chef to pre-cook the food for the grand finale. Julia, like Jean before her, would take her viewers through the cooking process, demonstrating how to blend the ingredients, and then, with a flourish, unveil the triumphant result. On that day in Channel 7's little studio in Dorcas Street South Melbourne Jean showed how to make a chocolate sponge. Like little children the crew and I longed to lick the utensils but had to wait…

Finally the credits rolled and we prepared to break the four-minute mile. In prime position to get there first (and before Mrs B could shout a warning) I'd grabbed my gobful. No plate, no fork, no niceties. We all got stuck into it.

Only to discover, too late, that the cream wasn't cream. It was the popular men's' hair-dressing of the era… Brylcreem.

To this day, 60 years later, I can still taste the foul muck.

Snakes Alive

Our three beloved dogs, Squire, CJ and Truffy, all dead within days of each other. Three graves side by side, adding to a pet cemetery that began four decades ago.

Squire, the patriarch, was one of very few Elmswood dogs to survive to an old age. One was run over by a neighbour. One was killed by a kangaroo.

We found Truffy the truffle-dog puppy – less than a year old – dying in the garden from a snake bite. Squire's daughter CJ died of unknown causes, but probably also a snake victim. That would make her the fifth to die that way. (Desperate dashes to the vets couldn't save them. Few dogs survive snakebite whereas, strangely, cats can.)

We've had many skirmishes with snakes. Protected species from which we need protection. Rory learned to crawl in close proximity to one – as discovered when moving a TV set. Presumably seeking warmth rather than entertainment. We found evidence of long-term residency in three shed skins.

I've lost count of snakes in the swimming pool – one there just last week. Though that'll be it for the year. Near-zero temperatures trigger hibernation. Which makes the deaths of Truffy and CJ all the sadder.

When Rory was little, Rory we used to swim in the billabong below the homestead and often found snakes swimming beside us. Mostly blacks or red-bellied blacks, deemed far less venomous than browns or tigers, amongst the world's deadliest. Although a neighbour damn near died from the bite of a black. He was climbing over a barbed wire fence when he felt something sharp and assumed he'd snagged his leg on a barb. It took a helicopter flight to John Hunter to save him.

We once found a small and very aggro tiger snake in the laundry. Managed to get a bucket over it. For fear of self-incrimination that story ends here. Another close encounter was beneath the swimming pool while, trying to clean a filter, I disturbed a brown that lunged at my face. Just missed. Very hard to tourniquet your head.

A farm worker sleeping in one of the cottages dreamt there was a snake in his bed. Awaking in terror he found there wasn't. But perhaps there had been. There was one under the bed. And later he found two in his 4WD farm truck that had managed to wriggle inside via the front wheel and a running board. Quite tricky removing them.

As it was removing eggs from a chook pen with snakes in residence. Two of them – one black and one brown, though folklore has them avoiding each other. Once again I shall avoid self-recrimination – but I managed to evict them, returning egg theft to the province of a huge goanna.

At last count I've ID'd six species of snake around the place, the sixth being small, very beautiful and hopefully non-deadly. But serious vipers and serpents don't only kill our pets. Cattle nosing through the grass can disturb a snoozing snakc and also fall victim.

You learn snake protocol. If you see one stand very still. Then walk slowly backwards. This doesn't always work. A particularly territorial boa constrictor once chased me for about twenty yards while I did a John Landy.

My advice. Don't have a Jack Russell as a farm dog. It'll confuse itself with a mongoose and take a snake on. And it'll lose. As two earlier graves attest.

And learn how to treat snakebite on humans.

Election Day

May 21. On this day, in 1930, Malcolm Fraser was born in toffy Toorak. He would become Australia's 22nd prime minister. These days he wouldn't get pre-selection.

Other notables sharing this birthdate include Princess Charlotte, Marylyn Monroe. Al Franken, Mr. T, Julius Caesar's mum, Fats Waller, Alexander Pope, Raymond Burr, Albrecht Durer, Philip II of Spain, Elizabeth Fry, Henri Rousseau, Andrei Sakharov, John Konrads, Leo Sayer and that nice Jeffrey Dahmer. It was the deathday for John Gielgud, Barbara Cartland and Rajiv Gandhi.

Great events on May 21? In 1927 Charles Lindbergh completed the first solo flight across the Atlantic. In 1932 Amelia Earheart became the first woman to do ditto. 1n 1972 Australian ratbag Lazlo Toth entered St Peters and modified a Michelangelo masterpiece with a mallet. In 1502 Joao De Nova discovered St Helena, future prison of Napoleon. In 1819 the first bicycle was introduced to NYC. I966? Muhammad Ali TKO'd Henry Cooper. 1981? Mittererand became President of France. In 1998 Suharto resigned as President of Indonesia.

And those two political changes reminds us that today, May 21st 2022 is… drum roll… a federal election.

We're told that the pen is mightier than the sword, though the continuing murder of journalists – by thugs including Putin – suggests otherwise. But today will illustrate that the pencil can be mightier than the pen. On the assumption that the tradition of marking the ballot with an HB pencil dangling on a piece of string in our voting booths continues, today we have the opportunity to mix metaphors by changing horses midstream or continuing on our merry way.

In either case, our weapon, opting for ballot over bullet, is that ceremonial pencil. Let the others have their voting machines where you pull levers in a political parody of the pokies. Here, this May 21st, 'tis a humble wooden pencil. Though our democracy does remain a gamble. (Joy oh joy! Queensland readers, for example, have a choice for the Senate that includes Pauline Hanson, George Christensen and Clive Palmer. What could possibly go wrong?)

I wouldn't dream of attempting to influence anyone's use of that all-powerful pencil. If you wish to prolong the political life of a government of unprecedented ineptitude – as demonstrated by the response to Covid and the slow-motion but accelerating catastrophe of climate change – go for it. If you're happy with ever more extreme weather events – droughts, floods and bushfires – you have candidates galore and a few entire parties to rely upon. If you like a government that produces enough financial scandals to keep a non-existent federal ICAC flat out forever – be my guest. A party that treats women wretchedly? Follow your nose – or hold your nose – and aim your HB accordingly. If you feel differently there are alternatives. And not just Albo's mob.

All the strings holding all the pencils can, in a sense, be woven into a rope to hang a parliament. (I've become quite partial to hung parliaments. Gillard proved they can be productive. And independents add interesting ingredients to the political recipe. So don't be timid about voting Teal).

A few weeks back this column told about me coming up with a slogan for that helped elect Moss Cass. 'I don't mind how you vote as long as you think about it.' That might not have been as potent or powerful as 'It's Time' but it had merit. So please think before you apply the pencil.

Laughter

As the crimson corpuscles continue to soak into the carpet it seems to this compassionate columnist that it's time to change the subject. To something light and frivolous. Laughter

Leaving aside the well-known comedians called Kookaburras (aka Laughing Jackasses) do others of God's creatures laugh, giggle or guffaw? It seems they do.

Whilst unknown among glum Gerard Hendersonians laughter is seen in other primates. Though diminishing numbers give them precious little to laugh about our evolutionary kin – the bonobos, chimpanzees, gorillas and orangutans – emit laugh-like vocalisations during play or when tickled. And we share the same ticklish places. Please take my word for it and do no experiment at home.

Experiments via sonographic studies also indicate that dogs laugh. Recordings of what seems to be dog laughter when replayed in laboratories to Labradors and other breeds promotes playfulness and tail wagging.

Ditto for dolphins. In 2004 Swedish researchers noticed 'short bursts of pulses followed by whistles'. Previously undetected, it became clear that the sounds were only emitted during play. I am currently training to replicate them at a local aquarium in the hope of communicating with a pod next summer.

Sadly, despite being so well equipped in the mouth and teeth department there is no evidence that sharks have a sense of humour.

The current count of comedians in animal species is 60. Including rats. Rats don't actually laugh but apparently they 'chirrup' when playing. Remember this the next time you hear a chirp. It may not be a rejoicing bird but a rollicking rat.

Twenty-odd years ago, in my scholarly introduction to that surprising best-seller (a million copies and counting) *The Penguin Book of Australian Jokes* I speculated on the origin of human laughter. It is my belief that it begins with the habit of tossing a hapless baby aloft – and what dad has not observed this ancient tradition.

It is also traditional to catch the baby. On the way up the baby inhales deeply in alarm. On being saved from the forces of gravity it emits a grateful grunt. That grunt, that gasp, that oomph of relief, is the first laugh. While taking nothing away from the hilarity observed amongst our hairy fellow travellers in their dwindling habitats in Africa or Indonesia, I believe that human laughter is of existential importance to us bipeds.

A few years after being launched into earth orbit by our fathers, humans are confronted by bad news: the inevitability of death. Enter stage right: religion. But not everyone buys the fairy stories of faith with its cheerful promise of heaven or the eternal, infernal flames of the basement.

And what choice do you have? Some respond by going nuts. Others seek oblivion in the bottle or less legal medications. But the more sensible amongst us choose the only proven antidote to despair and the acknowledged 'best medicine'... laughter.

When the alternative is the screaming abdabs, a diagnosis unknown to doctors that even the illustrious *Oxford Dictionary* concedes is lost in the mysterious mists of time, surely a cheerful chuckle is the best option? A vocal counterpart to giving the Grim Reaper the middle finger?

So here we are in a world of elections, inflation, wars in Ukraine, Covid, monkey-pox, extreme weather events, UFO surveillance and, worst of all, the possibility of Trump back in the White House. We have a choice of screaming or laughing.

I vote for laughter, even if desperate or strained.

Failed State

Once upon a time there was a magic kingdom. No, that's Disneyland. A magic republic. Proud of its constitution and believing in a manifest destiny. Then something went wrong and it lived unhappily ever after. To be more accurate a lot of things went wrong – and like many an imperial power before it – from the Roman to the British and the Soviet – it fell. The United States no more. It is a failed state.

A departing President, once a warrior, warned the people that their nation was in the power of what he called 'the military industrial complex' – an unholy alliance of the most vested of interests that has kept the US at war for most of its history – wars mostly on the wrong side of history. But it had been at war with itself even earlier – a so-called Civil War that cost over 800,000 deaths. A war fought largely over slavery, the great atrocity perpetrated on four million Africans – at a time when the total population was about the same as Australia's. And that war rages on – as judged by the ongoing destruction of black lives – and mass incarceration.

And there are ongoing massacres everywhere – 246 in a recent 22 weeks and all too often of schoolchildren – as a direct consequence of a wilful misreading of the sacred constitution orchestrated by an all-powerful terrorist organisation called the National Rifle Association that turns politicians into puppets. The citizenry own 400,000,000 guns – and not even presidential assassinations or Sandy Hooks or Uvaldes – will lead to significant disarming.

While living children remain targets unborn children will be 'protected'. Thanks to a Supreme Court stacked by Trump and his

Republican predecessors, abortion will be re-criminalized. Already red states are passing legislation than will charge doctors and pregnant women as murderers. It won't stop desperate women seeking terminations. It will simply make them far, far more dangerous. In many senses of the word.

On the one hand US science gave us the most effective Covid treatments. On the other the Trump regime so bungled its response to the pandemic that over a million people died. And Washington DC is the HQ for the climate change denialism that dooms millions more. Where once many in the world looked to the US for leadership now it shocks and awes with its fatal and fanatical stupidities. (Covid? 'Drink detergent' says Putin's president. Democracy? 'Drink my Kool-Aid').

Back to murder – US 'death rows' are full of men, mainly of colour, awaiting execution. While the penal system groans beneath the weight of grotesque drug laws.

From reason to treason. The most venial and corrupt president in US history – this against some stiff competition – tried to orchestrate the violent overthrow of what's left of lawful, legal US government. And yet Trump may regain power – his puppets poised to regain power in both houses in the looming midterms. And the world looks on in disbelief and fascinated horror.

This is a country all but defined by ultra violence, in its media and on its streets. The country with far and away the world's mightiest armoury of nuclear weapons, the only nation to use them – two in rapid succession. Relaxed and comfortable with Trump's regaining possession of the nuclear football? Trump's finger on the more than metaphoric button?

Biden may be but a brief road-hump in the ongoing momentum to US demagoguery. Welcome to the world of populism – courtesy the Dutertes, Bolsonaros, Modis, Putins and Trumps. Welcome to the age of Failed States.

John Clarke

John Clarke did not merely share the initials of Our Lord. The JC from New Zealand, like the JC of the New Testament, was something of a saviour. During many dark days John's gentle humour was a saving grace, greatly missed during the years of Scomo.

And John's humour was gentle. There's often cruelty in comedy but none in his. A memory: Clarkie and I went to the opening night of a one-man-show by another acknowledged genius and were numbed by the savagery, the sadism of the satire. Never a hint of that in *The Gillies Report* or *Clarke and Dawe.*

We'd first met in London in 1970 when filming *The Adventures of Barry McKenzie*. John's screen debut? A bit part playing one of the Australian Ockers from Earls Court. Returning home John devised another Bazza-style naïve in Fred Dagg and, almost overnight, became the most celebrated New Zealander since Edmund Hillary. But John found his new-found fame oppressive and sought asylum and anonymity in Australia.

Where I gave him a job at Adams Packer Films. One of our projects, Paul Cox's feature *Lonely Hearts*. Paulus Henrique Ignatius Cox was the most dour of Dutchmen and I despaired of his first draft. John's job was to brighten it up – and when he read his rewrite aloud to us even Paul, who'd resented the enforced collaboration, roared in laughter. Whereupon he begged John to take over from Norman Kaye in the lead with Wendy Hughes. Still shunning the spotlight John declined. *Lonely Hearts* went on to win the AFI's Best Film in1982. Meanwhile John became famous all over again via *The Gillies Report.*

Now to the next film we worked on. In the early days of our film renaissance Australia had no internationally recognized big name stars. Mel, Jack, Nicole, Cate and Judi were years away. So in the rough-and-tumble of the Cannes meat market we weren't in the running. Hence my idea of 'Blockbuster', a satire on the star system. And Clarkie joined me in the putative project.

Along the lines of Mel Brooks' *The Producers* our 'Blockbuster' would be a scam production. A young Aussie filmmaker would arrive on the Cannes' Croisette hawking a movie starring every imaginable marquee name living and dead. Elvis Presley. Marilyn Monroe, Grace Kelly, Clarke Gable etc, etc. All present and correct – namesakes recruited from the pages of the Melbourne and Sydney phonebooks. JC and PA found VIPs by the dozen.

The fact is we were spoiled for choices. The White Pages had, for example, a couple of Elvises and three Grace Kellys. Whether via the christening font or the deed-poll didn't matter to us. We could round them up, ship them over and completely confuse the paparazzi and the public on any red carpet you cared to roll out. And if not legit all perfectly legal.

From Blockbuster to Lacklustre. John and I played at movie moguls in our spare time – but by the time we'd a filmable film-script Hollywood history had not only caught up with us but zoomed past. Gibson, Thompson, Davis, Blanchett and Kidman were all Oscar-winning names in the pavement of Hollywood Boulevard, soon to be crowded by Jackman, Robbie, Bana, Rush, Hemsworth, Weaving, Ledger, Collette and that fellow exile from Clarke's New Zealand, Crowe.

Don't even have a copy of the script anymore. I think John's daughters do. But I tell you what. It's the funniest film we never made.

Oz Movies

It is all but forgotten that the movie industry began in Australia with a feature about Ned Kelly. And that business boomed until local production was effectively destroyed by the US and UK cinema owners. Then, in the 1960s there was a stirring. Some of us wanted to make films. Filmmakers' Cooperatives were formed producing 'Underground movies'. I made a few myself.

Cut to the most influential words I'd ever write – a one-page report to Prime Minister John Gorton. A blueprint for reviving the dead and buried Australian film industry. It began with a nod to US cultural dominance – aka 'coca-colinisation'.

'We hold these truths to be self-evident. It is time to see our own landscapes, hear our own voices an dream our own dreams'.

Gorton accepted my three recommendations and McMahon and Whitlam completed the job. Firstly, an 'Experimental Film Fund' would scatter some bread on the water, to see what young talent was out there. The best and brightest would be welcomed at a National Film and Television School and the graduates financed by a film bank – an Australian Film Development Corporation. Simultaneously I persuaded Premier Dunstan to establish a South Australian Film Commission – an innovation copied by most states – and we were off and running.

Within a few short years we were the darlings of the international festival circuit. At the vulgar end of the production schedule Bruce Beresford, Barry Humphries and I made the dreaded *Bazza* while Tim Burstall filmed *Alvin Purple*. At the posh end – two SAFC films – Ken Hannam's *Sunday Too Far Away* and Peter Weir's *Picnic at Hanging Rock*. The rest, as they say, is history.

Until that time few Australian actors had played an Australian on screen or stage – yet most 'do accents' for Noel Coward, Tennessee Williams or Arthur Miller. Australians were entirely familiar with the streets of NYC or LA but rarely glimpsed Melbourne or Sydney. We were drowning in American 'soft power' and knew American and British history better than our own. Australian kids had only American heroes. We were completely 'coca-colonised'.

I'd spend much of my life fighting against this foreign domination whilst dreading the prospect of Australia becoming a 'back lot' for the US using our studios, actors and crews as cheap labour, adding cost pressures on truly local films. I lost. They won. And Australian governments spend millions bribing the US studios to work here.

When I wrote that report for Gorton \$97 out of every \$100 spent at our box office went to an American film – leaving \$3 for everyone else in world – the English, Europeans and, yes, Australians. Crumbs from the US table. Factor in the streaming services the situation today is probably worse. A few brave souls make low budget Australian films – including a significant group of First Nations directors working miracles. But their films remain strangers in our own cinemas. And on Netflix and its ilk.

Which is why it saddens me to see Lurhmann's *Elvis*, like his overblown *Gatsby*, celebrated as an Australian film – with local actors playing Americans in mimicked accents. Hollywood, 'the dream factory', remains our dream factory. Largely created by Jewish refugees fleeing pogroms it has long welcomed filmmakers fleeing tyranny – or the big names in Australian acting, directing and cinematography seeking success on a grander scale. Fine. Great. But.

I hold these truths to be self-evident. More than ever, it is time to see our own landscapes, hear our own voices and dream our own dreams.

Top Gun

You may recall that a few months ago Scott Morrison lost office. Lost it? That sounds like a minor mishap, as though he'd mislaid the Lodge like an umbrella. In truth, he was well and truly kicked out. The voters told him to get lost.

One of the first things he did was to hire an entire cinema for a private screening of the Tom Cruise movie *Top Gun: Maverick*. Our no-longer top gun invited a few close mates and apparatchiks along for the fun. Its nice to think of them sitting in the dark munching popcorn along with the pop culture.

It illustrates a central concern I've been writing about for decades. The power of soft power. The way US dominance of cinema helped US dominance full stop. For generations over 97% of Australian cinema tickets went for American movies. Britain was shoved aside by Hollywood as we swapped the cultural cringe for 'coca-colonisation'. We lost our distinctions by osmosis. Even our colloquialisms were lost to those drongos. Sorry, those S.O.Bs. Our heroes were their heroes. Forget Ned Kelly – here's Hopalong Cassidy.

It was even worse with television. While the ABC rolled out the red carpet for BBC programs the commercial networks gave us the choice between American and American – Los Angeles versus New York. We dragged the Trojan Horse of US soft power into our very loungerooms. Law and Order wasn't just the name of a NYC drama. It became a term deployed in our elections, a way of thought. For many the US flag became their flag. Top Gun anybody?

Buy US culture today!! Free bonus offer!! US religiosity!! Forget fusty old-fashioned faiths like RC and CoE. Why speak Latin when you can speak in tongues! Swap to the new brands of Pentacostalism.

Sample QAnon! Listen to John Laws and Alan Jones mimic Rush Limbaugh. Turn our elections into de-facto US-style Presidential elections. Do selfies with Donald.

Soft power becomes indistinguishable from power power. Having another war? Please Mr President. Please! Can we come? Vietnam, Iraq? Your enemies are our enemies. Yes, we'll be on the wrong side of history, complicit in the murder of millions, but what are friends for?

Nor does it matter if we go to US wars based entirely on lies. Remember the fictitious Tonkin incident? Iraq's non-existent WMDs? Its central role in 9/11? Hollywood isn't the only dream factory. Try Washington DC.

Has the Supreme Court nuked Roe v Wade? Time for our Little-Sir-Echoes to raise the flag of the Australian confederacy. I exaggerate? Hardly. The drums are beating. Just as we couldn't wait to sign up for that most insane of public policies, the War on Drugs. If the US says 'jump!' we, almost without exception, ask 'how high?'

Any fraying vestigial links with King Charles III aren't our real problem. Our republican movement should be concerned with our domination by the US Republic. By the real-political fact that our head of state lives in the White House, not Buckingham Palace.

Our appetite for the US is insatiable. It's not just Maccas. When religious nutters invented Cornflakes in Battle Creek we munched them in millions of tonnes. We drink enough Coke to flood the Murray-Darling and Australia was the biggest world-capita market for Marlboro.

As the 51st state we at very least deserve a star on Old Glory. And a vote in the next presidential election.

See you at the movies.

Cinema Violence

In 1971, eight years before their brilliant *Mad Max*, George Miller and Byron Kennedy made *Violence in the Cinema Part 1*. It was a mockumentary with Arthur Dignam at a lectern admonishing filmmakers for the escalation of the 'pornography of violence' that he feared was exacerbating bad behaviour – arguing the same causality we saw between smoking and cancer.

As Arthur droned on he was shot, stabbed, mutilated and finally eviscerated – yet kept droning on. I took it personally because Arthur was re-enacting a speech I'd given to a Melbourne conference of psychiatrists and psychoanalysts.

What George Miller was mocking fifty years ago remains my view today: that the savageries depicted in film (and now participated in via video games) encourages brutal behaviour. This view is still mocked, dismissed as a form of wowserism, but is not offered as an argument for censorship. It calls for more responsibility from those in the so-called entertainment business

Appalled by the inventive sadism in *Mad Max* I acknowledged Miller's directorial skills. George's genius only made it worse. They mocked me again – Kennedy-Miller quoting my tut-tutting in their ad campaign. And they got the last laugh by turning the film into 'a franchise' that has enjoyed rave reviews and huge success.

Oddly enough I'd some support from Stanley Kubrick who coined the term 'ultra violence' for the surreal satire of *Clockwork Orange*. When seeing the behaviour of his Droogs mimicked in the mean streets of the UK Kubrick withdrew the film from circulation.

The first reaction to 9/11 was to think we were watching a replay of a Hollywood disaster movie. When George W Bush launched his insane war on Iraq many noted the similarities between the 'shock–and-awe' attacks on Baghdad and ultra-violent visuals of video games. Both were extrapolations of my argument that fictions can provide at very least the inspiration for real events. If not creating the violence, then certainly providing the choreography.

(I'm old enough to remember how Marlon Brando's *The Wild Ones* inspired local bikers – how James Dean's *Rebel Without a Cause* made 'playing chicken' popular on Australian roads. At the time a Bruce Petty cartoon of people watching the telly suggested we 'have our lives lived by American experts').

I've long lost both the battle and war. Now ultra violence is normal, at very least dulling our sensibilities, inuring us to it in real life. *Mad Max*'s big budget sequels and prequels are evermore innovative in their spectacle – a bit like the escalation of cruelties in the Roman Colosseum. And it's thumbs up to the thumbs down. Deaths in the arena or on the screen are so amusing.

In the dawn of cinema an image of an approaching steam train was enough to make the audience scream in terror. In recent decades it's needed a chainsaw massacre or slashing scissors in a Hitchcock shower scene. Watching a recent example of Miller mayhem I heard the audience roaring with laughter. Dulled sensibilities anyone?

I concede that news footage is even worse. And I repeat that I'm not advocating censorship – seeing the censor's scissors as more dangerous than Hitchcock's. In historical terms they've been weapons of mass destruction.

But isn't it time to stop playing chicken? To take the foot off the cinematic accelerator? So though stabbed, shot and eviscerated, so quaintly old-fashioned, I drone on.

Mikhail

With Mikhail Gorbachev's death at 92 it was time to dig out our 2006 pas-de-deux from the ABC archives, at least as deep as the KGB's. Though given the essential presence of his lifetime interpreter Pavel Pavlyuchenko it was a threesome.

My first trip to the Soviet was with Barry Jones, during a circumnavigation of the planet for PM Gorton collecting ideas to revive our film industry. Moscow day one: Comrade Jones and are seen on the cover of Pravda – outside the Kremlin throwing snowballs at each other. Moscow day two? We're in a Moscow jail – but that's another of those 'another stories'.

I'd made a few equally eventful trips to the USSR of the Cold War before returning to Moscow for Gorby's Perestroika and Glasnost. Yet it was in Brisbane I finally got to talk to him – before, during and after an hour-long chat.

Gorby was in town to promote Green Cross, his NGO with environmental ambitions. We stayed on the same floor of the same hotel and I remember being woken at 3am by an Irish woman (on the short list for a Nobel Peace Prize) hammering on his door and begging, unsuccessfully for admission. Whilst loathed in Russia everyone wanted a piece of him in the West.

Our formal chat began thus: 'This is one ex-Communist talking to another ex-Communist'. Gorby responded with a chuckle and, 'Yes, we are both social democrats now!' Sitting between us, holding a cheap Russian watch in his hands as if begging the hour to pass quickly, Pavel translated without lifting his eyes. I noticed he'd often answer for Gorby before Gorby.

And why not? He'd heard it all before, a hundred times. Torvill to his boss's Dean he'd even go-betweened between Gorby and Reagan. I joked to Gorby that we leave the whole thing to Pavel and go outside for a Balkan Sobranie.

Podcast the interview for all the content. Let me observe here that Gorby reminded me of Bob Hawke – another charismatic leader who, not content to invading your personal space, (standing so close you suffocate on the fumes of his aftershave) while insisting on a manly cuddle. I'm told Bill Clinton's the same.

All three cuddlers were the same brand of political fixers – except Gorby's attempts to fix the Soviet broke it into pieces. Which is why he was not greatly mourned by Putin who wants to glue it back again. The invasion of Ukraine – opposed by Gorbachev – is a bloodied piece of that jigsaw.

At the time of our Green Cross encounter Gorbachev was living in Moscow on a humiliatingly small pension. In the West he could earn millions on the speakers circuit and improve his cash flow by doing TV spots for luxury luggage and Pizza Hut. All the profits went into Green Cross and the Gorbachev Foundation. Whilst unintentionally destroying the Soviet Mikhail Gorbachev ended, at least for the time being, the Cold War and tried his best to rid the world of nuclear weapons. Chernobyl happened on his watch – so he had a heightened awareness of climate threats. Thus a bloke who started off as a party hack rose to become of the most significant figures in modern history.

But the wreck of the Soviet was not gratefully received by the millions he'd freed. Russians were afflicted by a collective PTSD – to such an extent that the average life expectancy, particularly for men dropped by years overnight. This is a world of unexpected consequences.

Vale Gorby.

Roo the Day

We've killed kangaroos in the millions. Yet they rarely harm one of us. A few weeks back a male pet badly injured a 77-year-old bloke and then prevented paramedics helping him. Police had to shoot the roo – but the man died. One of the few recorded cases in Australian history,

Having been bailed up by an angry Eastern Grey I am well aware that kangas can be very wild animals. Our standoff lasted fifteen fraught minutes and ended with me backing off. Very very slowly. A fully-grown boomer like him is over 2 metres tall and weighs 90 kilos.

A mob's dominant male gets used to fighting for its life. Forget the boxing kangaroos of sideshows and sporting flags. It's not the paws that hurt. Younger challengers can cause serious internal injuries – even disembowelment – with their huge hind legs. And while we've lost most of our dogs to snakebite, an Eastern Grey killed one of my favourites, when George was silly enough to confront him. Sometimes kangaroos will lead chasing dogs into dams and drown them.

I bottle-fed an orphaned joey I'd found beside her dead mother. Once persuaded of my good intentions she'd follow me everywhere like a puppy, curling up in an old skivvy at night. She'd hop under the shower with me – and travelled to and fro from Sydney sitting beside me on the front seat. Then hopping around the 2UE studios to the shock of fellow shock-jocks John Laws and Alan Jones. Memorably she peed all over one of Paul Keating's Zegna suits when he was giving her a Prime Ministerial cuddle while posing for a photo with a Chinese cultural delegation.

Nearing puberty she started to disappear for odd days, then for an entire week. Finally the call of the wild finally won. It was a sad day when she left to re-join the mob.

But this is about an even sadder day. I'd arrived back at the farm from Sydney at my usual time of 3am – to discover a fully-grown kangaroo in the garage. The old fella wasn't in good working order – clearly he'd lost the battle to a young buck. And against every instinct he'd braved dogs and got through fences to seek haven with humans. Not that he was friendly. My tentatively approached had him rearing up, ready to fight.

A mystery. Was it possible he'd been a pet? We phoned around the neighbours. 'Nobody raises a male. Too bloody dangerous.'

It was far from the only mysterious encounter. A few farms up the road friends Sandy and Mandy Archibald had a mob of white kangaroos. Not albinos. Just white. So much for evolutionary theory. How the hell had they survived?

With thousands sharing our 10,000 rugged acres (five distinct species of roo, wallaby and wallaroo) I've spent decades observing them. On one occasion my 6-year-old daughter Rory and I encountered a totally blind kangaroo. Totally deaf.

Petty

Picture in your mind this *New Yorker* cartoon. It's dark and we see the distant lights of Manhattan. In the foreground, having rolled all the way from the city and coming to a halt beside a remote farmhouse (and full of bewildered people) is a Ferris Wheel. A passenger climbs out and asks 'May we use your phone?"

And that, almost 70 years ago, is how I first encountered Bruce Petty. Australia has produced so many significant cartoonists. An official Hall of Fame includes Stan Cross, Will Dyson, Bill Leak, Emile Mercier, Alan Moir, Mike Leunig, Pat Oliphant, Paul Rigby, Cathy Wilcock, Ron Tanberg, Les Tanner, Patrick Cook, Peter Nicholson, Ward O'Neill, John Spooner, the Hogarthian David Rowe and more. All drawing brilliant conclusions. But at the pinnacle – and many of the living on the list – would agree, Bruce is the maestro. Petty by name but not by nature.

Yet when Bruce arrived back after considerable international success (the *New Yorker* was just one of the posh mastheads) he couldn't get a job. Editors would say 'My kid can draw better than that'. So he finished up working part-time in an ad agency when TV was just beginning. Whereupon we collaborated on one of the first animated TV ads. His squiggles to my lyrics. A jingle for Mobiloil. I can still sing it … 'big cars, bubble cars, trouble trucks and aeroplanes – steamrollers, rollercoasters, trams and trains'. Well, I was only sixteen. And I can still see it… with Bruce's variety of vehicles.

This led us to collaborate on *Hearts and Minds*, a film on the Vietnam War that won a major AFI Award. By then there was no stoping him. He went on to win an Oscar.

After filming in Vietnam Bruce came back from Vietnam profoundly changed. He didn't need an entire film to tell the story. He'd do that in just one great cartoon – in a new newspaper called *The Australian*. It showed two Vietnamese kids huddling in a landscape blasted by bombs and napalm. One kid says to the other 'What are you going to do if you grow up'.

If.

We'd grown up a just few miles from each other – me on a small farm in East Kew and he on one in Doncaster. And our lives would keep intersecting. He persuade legendary editor Adrian Deamer to give me a job at *The Oz* – and decades later I'd return the compliment by having another legendary editor in Graham Perkin offer Petty political-cartoonist asylum at *The Age*. Over the years I'd write intros for a Bruce book and he'd illustrate one of mine. Quite a few Pettys hang on my office wall. Including costume designs for a Shakespearian production at the Old Vic.

Bruce's body of work includes other award-winning films – on art, Australian history and Karl Marx. He also built unwieldy, wondrous and wobbly machines, all interconnected cogs and levers, to dramatize the connectedness between people and policies. Political and environmental.

Why this column now? For the simple reason that Bruce turns 93 in November – he' still drawing – and I knew you'd want to know. To hell with state funerals – we should have state birthdays. And not only for royalty.

Before letting you get on with your day – a memory of another Petty masterpiece. This time wordless. Drawn in honour of the Dismissal, it's a simple sketch of Parliament House (the old one) with a huge fan on top.

What's that hitting it?

Happy

'If you're happy and you know it, clap your hands!' Thus urges the nursery rhyme – and there are scores of renditions on YouTube, some sourced from Sesame Street. However, the lyrics seem to derive from Latvia whilst the tune closely resembles a song written for a Soviet film called Volga-Volga. Very few in the USSR were clapping with happiness at the time. It was 1938.

And very few in Russia will be clapping their hands currently. Putin's invasion of Ukraine and his mobilisation have not been happy decisions.

In any case Putin must know that happiness is an American plot. Its pursuit in their Constitution makes it both official and compulsory. At this time, when we're reconsidering ours and have so many causes for unhappiness (pandemics, politics, the weather etc) perhaps we should consider another borrowing from the US – like our foreign policies, our wars on drugs and much of our popular culture. Australians all let us rejoice and pursue happiness.

Let me quote from the US original. Here's how the Founding Fathers made fun official. Drum roll if you please.

'We hold these truths to be self-evident, that all men are created equal, that they are endowed by their Creator with certain unalienable Rights, that amongst these are Life, Liberty and the pursuit of Happiness'.

That was difficult when weighted down with the chains of slavery – frequently used by the FFs to prevent their fully-owned humans from pursuing Liberty in any form. So much for being created equal, but it was a lovely sentiment.

And Americans, at least unchained ones, have always pursued happiness. They build Disneylands to monetise it (even more than happiness the US sanctifies the pursuit of profit). Not that you need theme parks. Every shopping mall offers the joys and jubilations of shopping. And nothing makes an American happier than shopping.

Except drugs. Behold a paradox. Here the official injunction to pursue happiness collides with prohibition – once limited to booze but now covering almost every form of happiness induced by unofficial plants. Naughty poppies for example, and tsk tsk marijuana. Pursing this sort of happiness leads to a loss of Liberty, particularly if you happen to be black.

You are however free to pursue happiness via guns. Of all sorts, big and little, up-to-and-including ballistic missiles, although some restrictions apply regarding nuclear warheads. No prohibitions here. You're at Liberty to lock and load. Indeed, you're encouraged to do so. If the NRA continues to get its way they'll be compulsory. How else will the US maintain its much-admired lead in massacres?

Some pursue happiness in fast cars. Some in what is best described in this family-friendly journal as the horizontal tango. (No mention of sex by the prime signatories of that solemn and sacred US document. But perhaps it was taken as read, another self-evident truth.) Many pursue it via gambling or gluttony or other of the deadly sins – or by defying the Commandments and coveting thy neighbour's ass. Different strokes.

I prefer the pleasures of prose – both reading and writing it. It is a quiet way to pursue happiness and although one rarely actually catches it the exercise is healthy and releases few greenhouse gasses.

I'll leave you now. Let you get on with it. Fearing that some of you will spend the arvo if not the entire weekend pursuing happiness via sport. Watching it, playing it or both. Have fun.

Vroom Vroom

The Great Divide in this country was not only a mountain range. Equally divisive were issues of race: the atrocities consequential to the lie of Terra Nullius, the bigotries enshrined in the White Australia Policy and our continuing mistreatment of refugees. Then came religion – the great divide between Catholics and Proddies that tore our politics apart for generations. And finally there were cars. The great divide between Ford and Holden.

Forget football codes. The war between the two auto brands seemed a permanent form of road rage, like Northern Ireland on wheels. When Australians chose sides, their automotive allegiances were passed down from generation to generation, loyalties as intense as patriotism. While one masquerading as 'Australia's own car' it seems appropriate that we were choosing between two American brands.

Now Holden, like the formal White Australia Policy, is gone. Removed from Australian culture by a decision made in Detroit. The Holden lion, once as Ozzie Ozzie Ozzie as the Qantas kangaroo, is road kill. Nowadays the only motorised vehicles manufactured here are motor mowers, a bit slow for the daily commute.

But other forms of automotive apartheid live on. Rear wheel versus front wheel versus 4WD. Ute versus sedan versus SUV. And petrol versus diesel versus electric. Each with its passionate devotees.

There've been attempts to power cars by solar – even long-distance racing between vehicles looking crustacean with their carapaces of rooftop panels. But they're now marginalised by the likes of Musk. A paradox given solar's triumph on the rooftops of our suburban homes. Given our sunburnt country will be increasingly sunburnt by climate change I'd have hoped CSIRO would be fighting for the sun as motive power.

My old cobber Dr Karl K came up with a great solar-powering idea yonks ago. Pointing out how our hot black asphalt roads in summer can make our highways, freeways and motorways into a vast solar grid. Already linked and interconnected to suburban roads!

Karl didn't suggest it, so I will. Don't electrify our cars. Electrify our roads! Like electric trams cars could just charge around without recharging. That electric Elon wouldn't like it is a powerful argument in its favour. Anything to reduce the menace of Musk. And KK and PA could share the Nobel Prize for Physics. Or Common Sense.

The original Tesla fought a long battle with Edison – his erstwhile employer – over the merits of AC versus DC. Nikola favoured Alternating Current over Thomas' Direct Current with grisly demonstrations involving executions of elephants and humans. Lacking an iota of electrical literacey I'll leave the final decision to Karl. But for all my ignorance I'm convinced this is the answer. Turning Australia's hot road into 'hot' roads. Self-drying roads too – that would be a doddle.

I expect to be mocked. That is the destiny of we true visionaries. But they mocked my mentor Jo Bjelke-Peterson too. Remember when Jo backed the Horvath hydrogen car? That was powered by water! Goodonyner Jo – who's laughing now?

I am entirely confident that a new car industry will rise from the ruins of Detroit – that GM executives reading this column will reopen rusty plants across Australia. Ditto Ford. And soon, once again, we will be choosing between Ford and Holden and give Musk a kick in the bum. The world's richest man no more. Elon will be humbled, reduced to thumbing a ride beside the electrified Hume Highway.

Next. Solar submarines.

Dictionary

Take this book in your right hand – or left if you're a molly-dooker – and say after me. 'This book contains all wisdom'.

However the volume in question is not *The Bible* but the dictionary. Preferably, The Dictionary, indisputably that masterpiece of scholarship, the *Oxford*. Running to dozens of heavy volumes the *Oxford* is too cumbersome to hold unless you possess a fork-lift. So perhaps one of its mini-sized versions will have to do. My point is that a decent dictionary contains enough of the English vocabulary, enough words in waiting, to contain an infinite number of novels, dramas, sonnets, essays, non-fiction books, personal letters etc etc.

A jig-saw puzzle can only be fitted together one way. The words in a dictionary? Put them together anyway you like – and voila! – a tweet or a newspaper column. Just as musical notes can create everything from an improvised jazz solo to Beethoven's 11th (or would've had Ludwig lived a little longer) words, words, words, (if you're not sick of them like Eliza Doolittle), have the same unlimited potential. Ask Shakespeare, Tolstoy or any other wordsmith. Shuffle them together in the right order, add punctuation and avoid plagiarism, and you're guaranteed a Booker, the Nobel Prize for Literature or both.

(There are, of course, other forms of language not included in a dictionary. The mysterious language of mathematics, needed by HSC students, or an Einstein, Hawking or other explorer of the infinite. Cosmology and quantum mechanics eschew words for numbers and symbols, for enigmatic equations squiggled on a backboard. Such language is entirely foreign to your author, yet to comprehend digital measurement).

For a history of The Dictionary I commend to you *The Surgeon of Crowthorne*, by that that paradigm of pen-pushers Simon Winchester. Or see the film version – *The Professor and the Madman*. The miracle of the *Oxford* will be revealed in all its improbabilities. Having made do with *The Shorter Oxford* or *The Concise,* Readers' Digest-style condensations, I finally lashed out and bought the real thing. It sits beside me in all its glory as I tap out these words, in a purpose-built wooden cabinet. I rarely refer to it but like to know its there in an emergency. A literary version of a fire-extinguisher or medicine cabinet. My first-born daughter, Dr Rebecca Adams, has demanded I leave it to her my will.

Simon explains its history with style – beginning with the 1857 call for a new English Dictionary – to take up where Samuel Johnson left off – by the Philological Society in London. Belatedly gaining momentum it was 'completed' in 1928, and since 1933 has been updated ever since. It became a CD-ROM in 1992 and is now being published on-line.

As if 273,000 words – 171,000 in current use – aren't enough. Newly minted words are constantly being added. Atrocities like pawternity leave, Brexit, QAnon, woke and cancel culture – and inevitably Covid-19, PPE, frontliners, lockdown, mask-up and anti-mask. The phrase Black Lives Matter arrived and conspiracy theory has had a resurgence. The definition of trump has been updated and variants added. (Note to self. Check to see how *Roget's Thesaurus*, that literary Tyrannosaurus, is getting on.)

Does the OED ever cancel words? The answer is an emphatic no. Where the dead were immediately dropped from the recently deceased *Who's Who* once a word appears in the *Oxford* it's there forever, fossilized in the geological layers of the English language. So, sadly, they will never dump Trump.

See you later.

The Crown

I blame myself completely. Why oh why didn't I contact Netflix before that interloper Peter Morgan? Then it would be me counting the royalties from royalty. By now I'd be rolling in the revenues from *The Crown* – as opposed to Morgan's half-a-crown version.

My dirt file dwarfs Pete's. I've known the name of HM's main mistress pre-dating Camilla (who just happens to have been an Australian) and oodles on when might be described as the Duke of Edinburgh's down-under doings. Furthermore I've spent quality time with the bloke about to be crowned King Charles III – and his then child-bride Princess Diana. Moreover I've shopped at Harrods.

Even now it's not too late – if Peter Morgan calls I'll give him juicier tit-bits than Queen Elizabeth fed the corgis. And all for a very modest fee. Just in time for the final series.

Kiss-and-telling might sound a bit crass, but they're not my kisses I'd be telling. If you're reading this Peter, here's a few nudge-nudge-wink-wink- say-no-more hints.

First, re a Duke who shall remain nameless. From time to time he'd arrive here on solo, queenless visits to advance his charities and sundry good works. And among his ducal dalliances were two I knew about. One with a woman I'll call Jean, one with someone I'll call Judith. As it happens that were their actual names.

A friend and colleague Jean, a renowned arts administrator, who felt duty bound to support the monarchy. The other was the wife of a prominent portrait painter who'd previously had an erotic encounter with you-know-who in London. I will say no more until the cheque clears.

Now to our next king. As I'm sure he vividly recalls, we met three times. Once at Government House in Canberra, one at Government House in Melbourne and one at the movies. Ditto Diana.

Invited to din-dins at Yarralumla in one of my official capacities (Chair of the Australian Film Commission) my wife and I were sitting at a little table with his blushing bride. And I use the word blushing advisedly. Every time I spoke to Di she'd blush. 'Please pass the sauce.' A blush. All over. This was clear given she was in a backless gown. I had to be very careful for fear she'd pass out.

(My main memory of our conversation? She told me HM's favourite TV show was *Kojak*. Whereas, with a blush, Di confessed to preferring *Dynasty*. Or was it *Dallas*? A few days ago this newspaper reported that towards the end of her long life the Queen was a regular viewer of *Line of Duty*, though she complained it was hard to follow the plot. I agree. Unfathomable.)

Cut to Gov House by the Melbourne Bot Gardens where we co-hosted a reception for local film identities – and I marvelled how the royal co-stars worked the room. Torville and Dean. Cut to that night at the movies – was it a screening of *The Man from Snowy River*? At His request I presented him with a king-size pack of DVDs of other Oz fillums, modestly not including my own epics *Barry McKenzie* and *Dons Party*. I shuddered at the thought of such vulgarity besmirching Buckingham Palace.

So Peter, ring me. It's not too late for a creative collaboration. Let me help end your series on the Saxe-Coburg and Gotha with a bang.

Fade to black.

In Black and White

Black deaths in custody? Recently we've had nationwide rallies provoked by the death of an Aboriginal child deemed to have been 'in the wrong place at the wrong time'. Time to look back over history.

White South Africans imposed apartheid on the black majority of its population in 1948. It ended in 1994. White Australians imposed the White Australia Policy in 1901 and it ended, finally, in 1973. Whitlam's decision remains an affront to many of our fellow citizens who, like Pauline, her Hansonites and other proud whites constantly try and revive White Australia – in their attitudes to refugees, for example, and their hostility to the Uluru Statement.

They have, of course both right and white on their side. Browns, yellows and particularly blacks are the wrong colour and have only themselves to blame. This is also true of the mixed-race people once known as half-castes – for whom Gina's dad Lang advocated mass sterilisation. This falls short of some form of myxo-for-humans, if you can call such people human, but Mr. Hancock was ever the moderate.

White is the superior colour, or lack of colour, for countless reasons. You see this in our symbolism and our language. White represents innocence, cleanliness, purity, virtue, brilliance – hence everything from Persil whiteness to the white wedding dress. There is no higher praise than 'You're a white man'. Ask any white-robed Klansman.

Black, on the other hand, is the colour of evil, death and mourning. Beware the black arts of the occult and moral turpitude. Think blackmail, black-hearted, blackguard, blackjacks, blacklegs, blackening the reputation. Think blacklist, blackballing, blackouts, a black mark, the black market.

You have been warned. Black is bad. The only time I can think the word black has a positive association is when something is clearly stated as 'in black and white' – or when you're 'in the black'. Elsewhere black is forever on the wrong side of the ledger.

Black and white can, of course, get on fine. Look at the keys on a piano. In the pre-colour, pre digital days it worked well for newspapers. And if sanity prevails and if we vote for the Voice centuries of injustice will be on the mend. The Voice is no attempt to impose a Black Australia Policy – simply a first step in giving First Nations people, yes, a voice.

In the sixties African Americans found it necessary to assert that 'black is beautiful' – more recently that 'black lives matter'. The word 'Negro – and hence 'the N-word'- comes from Spain and Portugal and helped brand Africans as 'the other' and justify their enslavement. To 'be sold down the river' – a reference to slave markets on the Mississippi. Locally? White Australians enslaved Pacific Islanders to work in our cane fields. That had the cheerful name of blackbirding.

Almost as cheerful was blackface – as American whites parodied African Americans – with Australian whites doing the same for blackfellas. Good clean fun. And no probs. It washed off.

If only we could wash the racism out of our history, our language, our symbolism and our very minds. Didn't Martin Luther King have a dream about that?

The fact that all humanity derives from black Africa doesn't cut it with white bigots. That's as heretical – as blasphemous – as telling white Christians that Jesus was brown.

The recent tragedy in Western Australia is symptomatic of a culture still in crisis. There remains a crying need for many a Sorry Day.

2023

Slang

Ages ago I started a Society for the Protection of Australian Slang – to ward off the onslaught of Americanisms. Clearly it was a total failure. So over the break I asked readers for favourite examples of Australian slang and rhyming slang – plus sundry colloquialisms and vulgarisms.

First cab off the rank – that phrase perhaps an example, was the extraordinary expression 'a wigwam for a goose's bridle'. Was it one of ours? And what could it possibly mean? In a sense it is meaningless, a term for something absurd. My researches discovered its origin was English but it gained currency in Australia from 1917. We were off to a flying start.

Many people liked drongo, an Australianism for fool or dill. (And yes, dill is also one of ours). I've always found drongo the most delightful of derogative terms because it contains a hint of affection.

Quite a few vulgarisms were, I suspect, coined by Barry Humphries for our charming fillum *The Adventures of Barry McKenzie*. 'I hope your chooks turn to emus and kick your dunny down,' and 'Go and stick your head up a dead bear's bum.' In Bruce Beresford's subtitled print of the film for British audiences that became, 'Thrust your cranium u the sphincter of a deceased bruin.'

Now to a random selection proffered by the public. And share with me a sense of loss that so many have been shoved aside by less poetic US imports. Any Dylan Thomas would be proud of their poetic imagery and rhythm.

Flat as a shit-carter's hat. Flat out like a lizard drinking. Better than a poke in the eye with a sharp stick. I'm so hungry I could bite the arse out of a low-flying duck. Silly as a hatful of handshakes. Couldn't pull the skin off a custard. Full as a State School hatrack. A few roos loose in the top paddock. A head like a half-sucked aniseed ball. A head like a robber's dog. About as useful as a chocolate teapot. Wouldn't know a tram was up him until the conductor rang the bell. I'll have your guts for garters. Whatyamacallit. You thought wrong. Couldn't raffle a duck in a country pub. Couldn't organise a piss-up in a brewery. You're getting on my quince. Running around like a blue-arsed fly. Face like the Northern end of a Southbound camel. Face like as kicked-in kero tin. Don't come the raw prawn with me. He was all over me like a rash. Dry as a pommy's towel. Wouldn't shout if a shark bit him. Happy as a bastard on Fathers Day. Donkey's years, yonkey's years, yonks. Stone the crows. Strike me rotten. Couldn't fight his way out of a wet paper bag. He's been doin' that since Jesus played full back for Jerusalem. Rattle your dags. Busier than a one-armed brickie in Beirut (???) Mad as a box of frogs. As flash as a rat with a gold tooth. Needs a good kick up the klacker. As useless as a two-bob watch. The drover's brekkie: a fart and a cigarette. Got the good clobber on.

Haven't the space for the richness of rhyming slang – a proud tradition we seem to have inherited from the Cockneys. Another wonderful realm of verbal creativity (e.g : after dark for shark, Jimmy Dancer for cancer). Or to list the long list of long lost words. But if you'd like to add to this scholarly collection write to me at philadams@ozemail.com.au and we might run a sequel.

See yers later.

Sunburnt

I love this sunburnt country
From Darwin to St. Kilda
From shearing shed to dunny
Let's all waltz our Matilda!

Where Slip Slop Slap
We wisely howl
While our national flag's
The Dicky's towel

I love this sunburnt country
Where just yesteryear
We'd redbacks on the toilet seat
'n got nagged by Germaine Greer

Where now the job of PM
Doesn't last a month of Sundays
Now we change them oft as socks
More often than our undies.

We're all deafened by cicadas
Plus endless pollie waffle
Let's pack 'em off to ICAC
Coz their snouts are in the truffle

I love this sunburnt country
Of droughts and flooding rain
Of kangas and koalas
Where football's on the brain

If you can kick or thwack a ball
Then you're one of us
For sport is our religion
No limit to the fuss

With shopping a close second
LikeBoxing day – a hurry.
Thank god for Bezos' Amazon
More Darling than the Murray

All hail Harvey an' Greg Norman
And Al and Barry Jones
A nation needs its heroes
As a body needs its bones.

The Bartys and the Seekers
And our lovely Johnny Farnham
Join me and clink the glasses
Provided by the barman.

Toss shrimps onto the barbie!
Less fear more cheer more beer!
Recent times were on the nose
2023? It'll be a vintage year

Forget the rising tolls
In ICU, Tunnel and Bridge.
Ignore pandemic variants
With a coldie from the fridge

I love a sunburnt country
With its rugged mountain ranges
Lets build mountains of coal
And forget the climate changes

(PS. If you love our country as it is
– then clearly make your choice.
Follow the NATS and Pauline H
And vote to veto the Voice.)

Favourite Films

Donald Trump has a favourite film. He demands his entourage watch it repeatedly. In the White House, on Air Force One and presumably in his fuehrer bunker in Florida – seemingly blind to the similarities between the central character and himself. Parodying the cult of celebrity, Billy Wilder focuses on a has-been movie star still convinced she's the centre of the universe.

While admiring *Sunset Boulevard* too my all-time favourite is Carol Reed's *The Third Man*. Set in post-war Vienna, Graham Greene's screenplay takes us from the heights of a giant Ferris Wheel to the depths of the city's sewers. Neither the cinematography by Australian Robert Krasker nor its zither theme by Anton Karas have been surpassed. Nor the central performance by Orson Welles. Nor its ending, the most haunting in cinema history.

What follows is no cinephile's list of ' best films' – only those I've most enjoyed.

Kubrick's *Paths of Glory* and *Space Odyssey*. Described by the sainted Stanley as 'the most beautiful movie ever made' Ridley Scott's *Blade Runner.* Coppola's *Apocalypse Now*. Most of the Coen Bros. Ditto the French New Wave, the Tati films and *Belle de Jour*.

The cancelled Woody Allen's *Annie Hall.* Donskoi's *The Gorky Trilogy* – which as Satyajit Ray told me – inspired his brilliant *Apu Trilogy*. Other Soviet efforts – *Battleship Potemkin*, *The Cranes are Flying*, *Andrei Rublev* and Bondarchuk's *War and Peace*.

Visconti's *The Leopard* and *Death in Venice*. David Lean's *Lawrence of Arabia* (naughty Noel Coward said Peter O'Toole was so pretty it should have been retitled Florence of Arabia). An entire festival of

Fellini's – like *8 ½* and *La Dolca Vita*. De Sica's *The Bicycle Thief*. Costa-Gravis' *Z*. Chaplin's *Modern Times* and *City Lights*. Keaton's *The General. The Red Shoes. The French Connection. Wake in Fright. Don't Look Now.* My highest-ranking horror film – James Whale's 1931 version of *Frankenstein*. Spielberg's *Duel*, his first and still his best – although his sci-fi extravaganza *Close Encounters* was a triumph.

Ugetsu. Rashomon. Singing in the Rain – with Kelly performing the title song among the most sublime sequences ever. *Oliver!* – directed by Carol 'Third Man' Reed – the best British musical. Four cheers for Ron Moody's *Fagin*. Menzel's *Closely Watched Trains* and Andrzej Wajda's *Kanal. A Night to Remember* – a 1958 b&w British film on the Titanic – vastly superior to Cameron's blockbuster. *The Right Stuff. Shane. The Maltese Falcon. 12 Angry Men.* Hated Elia Kazan's 's politics but oh, his *On the Waterfront, America America!* and *East of Eden. The Seventh Seal. The Life of Brian. Moulin Rouge* – John Huston's, not Baz Luhrmann's bloated effort. *The Great Gatsby* – Jack Clayton's not Baz's. Peter Weir? *Picnic at Hanging Rock* and his masterpiece *The Truman Show*. Schepisi's *Chant of Jimmy Blacksmith*. Phil Noyce's *Rabbit Proof Fence*. Warwick Thornton's *Samson and Delilah* and *Sweet Country*.

Favourite Hitchcocks? *North by North West* and *Rear Window* – which eerily I last saw sitting beside an ancient James Stewart. Another Wilder – *Some Like it Hot* – with the second best-ever film ending. The UK's *The Long Good Friday* – third best.

Citizen Kane? Compulsory. *Casablanca* ditto, despite its crappy back-lot sets – not so much for Bogart and Bergman but a few magical seconds of dialogue. Hoping for a new home in the US two elderly Jewish refugees practise telling the time in English. 'Vot votch?' 'Ten votch.' 'Such much?'

And it's time to stop. While you think of your list.

Pyramid Scheme

Over the years I've juggled many careers. As well as farmer, filmmaker, columnist, communist, broadcaster, ad man, political apparatchik and drug dealer I've delivered newspapers with a billycart and telegrams on a clunky red Post Office bicycle. But my most important work has gone unremarked. My contributions to archaeology.

It was me, after all, who realised that Easter Island was covered in giant statues of Malcolm Fraser. All his greyness and gloom perfectly captured. And note that the looming figures are trouserless. How the ancient islanders could predict Malcolm's sartorial predicament is best left to the speculations of Erik von Daniken, the author of *Chariots of the Gods*, which reveals the Pyramids were built by aliens.

Which leads to my greatest discovery: Ancient Egypt's pyramid scheme. Having built lots of these Toblerone tombs up and down the Nile (the grand total from Kush to Cairo nudges 200) it was time to export the aliens' technology. Funded by the Pharaohs some adventurous Egyptians set sail in a flotilla of reed-rafts with Mesoamerica on their minds. The market potential! All those Aztecs and Incans without a clue how of how to build them.

Forget Cook, Dampier and those other wannabees. 70,000 years after the First Nations it was the Ancient Egyptians who stumbled across Australia. Blown off course by bad weather they found themselves up the creek without a paddle. At what is now the postal address for Melbourne.

To keep themselves in practise the Gippos promptly built a tiny pyramid, Australia's one-and-only, recently repurposed by the ANZACS (no relation to the Aztecs) as the Shrine of Remembrance.

And when they were finished they stood on the banks of the aforementioned creek, hardly a threat to the might of the Nile, and exalted their principle deity Ra. 'Yea Ra!' they called out. And yes, that's how the Yarra got its name.

Then off they went and the rest is history. Business boomed and at the last pyramidal census there were, Scout's honour, 2,000 in the Americas. From the US to Peru.

Some party-pooping academics pooh-poo my discoveries. As they did the hypothesis of my friend Eric Von Daniken. But how else can they explain the other signs of their local presence?

It is well known that the Ancient Egyptians brewed the first beer, based on the fermentation of a yeasty brew made from bread. The hieroglyphic record says it was called 'peor'. Thus beer would become Melbourne's favourite drink. And don't get me started on the obelisk by Sydney's Hyde Park.

There was also some intermarriage – or if not marriage acts of sexual congress. Ask Fred Nile.

Easter Island. The Shrine. The Yarra. So much discovered, to little to show for it. Apart from an Hon Doc from Macquarie – the Uni with the best Egyptian department in the country.

With my use-by date (and hence my mummification) rapidly approaching I can't see myself returning to my spiritual home of Egypt in the immediate future. There's so little of it. So do me a favour. Next time your visiting the Big Three across the river from Cairo please give the Sphinx a fond pat on its bottom and say 'hi'. Or 'yea Ra'.

PS. Guess where our Elmswood homestead stands? As proud as a pyramid? On the Isis River. Spooky? Then what about the fact that Malcolm losing his daks in Memphis? Which happens to be the name of an Ancient Egyptian capital. The prosecution rests.

The Tree

'I think that I shall never see a poem lovely as a tree' quoth arboreal enthusiast Joyce Kilmer (1886-1918). And Joyce was just warming up. The poem went on to talk of said tree 'lifting its leafy arms to God to pray'. Hopefully his tree was a Christian praising the approved deity.

Warren Buffet is another fan. 'Someone is sitting in the shade today because someone planted a tree a long time ago'. Moved Warren, seconded Ralph, as in Waldo Emerson. 'The creation of a thousand forests is in one acorn.' And Thoreau tells of taking a walk in the woods and 'coming out taller than the trees'.

I'm particularly fond of the story that casts Von Bismarck as a pioneer tree hugger. Apparently Otto would leave a claustrophobic meeting to embrace an oak or elm, finding this spiritually nourishing. Spike Milligan would take this manly embrace one stage further by singing 'I talk to the trees – that's why they put me away'.

I too raise my non-leafy arms to pray – for trees. A friend sent me a photograph of the tiny farm where my grandparents raised me. And there it stood, by the rickety front gate: the tree that was my best friend in early childhood. Nothing grand, just a gnarled, scruffy, middle-sized peppercorn that I loved to climb, finding comfort in its leafy arms. Even though I once fell out of it and, 80 years later, still have a scar to prove it.

I'd sit up there looking down on a world where horsepower still meant horses. Grandpa's draught horse Blossom pulled his plough, and horses delivered bread, milk, ice and, in winter, firewood. I'd watch the comings-and-goings plus observing the toings-and-froings of Number 48 trams.

I really loved my old tree. Even if its bark was rougher than sandpaper it was gentle and seemed to return my affection. Long gone of course – as is the farm itself. (A few years later it was divvied up into housing blocks, the houses themselves now in their dotage). But if you're in tune with trees yourself – and in the vicinity of what was 798 High Street East Kew you might sense its ghostly presence.

Other trees became friends in later years – I'm still on good terms with a few at my farm today. Those, that is, that survived the cataclysmic hurricane that ring-barked and uprooted a thousand – and, far worse, the last great drought. Thousands didn't make it, and their uplifted arms are bare and skeletal.

We should pray for trees – for the loss of arboreal lives in drought, bushfires, land-clearing and climate change. And follow Buffet's advice and invest in them. According to one Nelson Henderson 'the true point of life is to plant trees under whose shade you do not expect to sit.' As Martin Luther said 'every green tree is more glorious than if it were made of gold or silver.'

So let's plant trees in their billions in the hope of saving the biodiversity only trees can protect – and so counter the maniacs like Brazil's tree butcher Bolsonaro. And give three cheers for photosynthesis.

The Greens don't go far enough. Hence my efforts to organise trees into a political party – without branch stacking. Join me in urging Tanya Plibersek to get them the vote.

Trees are the oldest living creatures on earth. He (or she) who plants one plants hope.

Reading

You are, at this very moment, reading. Congratulations. You are, by definition, literate. And reading is, in principle, a good thing to do. Unless you're a German in the 1930s reading *Mein Kampf*. In that case stop immediately and burn your copy. It's OK, even if you're a Nazi. Hitler went on to encourage book burning.

Reading this column is strongly recommended, at least by the columnist – along with newspapers in general which I recommend you do in the old-fashioned form where newspapers are actually paper.

Call me sentimental, but my first job in the media was a paperboy.

You should also read product labels, medical instructions, road warnings and, of course, books. Books, that is, other than Hitler's. Although it is permissible to have books read to you in the form of audiobooks as I do on my long commutes. I'm currently listening to fellow atheist Richard Dawkins being rude about God, but you might prefer that marvellous work of fiction, *The Bible*.

Books have been around for yonks, perhaps even longer than yonks. Their story begins before most humans could read – with an invention called the Codex. Codices (that's plural, if your library contained more than one) replaced papyrus scroll. (Odd that now, yonks later, we're back to scrolling.) It was a radical idea – to bind single pages together, so you could have chapters and, in the last pages, an index. Rolling through a lengthy scroll was not only time-consuming and very tiring but it was hard to find what you were looking for. Imagine the thickness of a scroll of *Harry Potter* or James Joyce's *Ulysses*.

In the golden olden days books were hand-made, usually by monks who spent their lives illustrating manuscripts. Thus a book cost oodles and oodles. The trouble really started when a bloke called Guttenberg nicked the idea of moveable type from the Chinese and began to print them. Suddenly books were everywhere, requiring the invention of shelving and library ladders, not to mention libraries. Books were both democratised and subjected to the tyrannies of the Dewey-decimal system.

The next great step was provided by a pommie called Sir Arthur Lane, the founder of Penguin Books. He invented the cheap paperback as opposed to the posh hardcover. Or as naughty Dame Edna prefers to call them 'limp versus stiff'. Suddenly everyone could afford a book, the riff and the raff. All that you needed was the ability to read, so there was an incentive to learn which may have led to the beginning of education. I'll have to check that on Wikipedia.

Mind you, you don't have to read if you just listen to audiobooks. You just have to listen, which requires no education at all. I hope you're taking notes as you'll be asked questions afterwards. Although that requires learning to write, another skill demanding education, although I'm sure there's an app for it.

I've got 40,000 books – piled up in room after room and a couple of repurposed 40-foot shipping containers. Almost every book I've read since William and Biggles, so loved and treasured, plus oodles sent to me over the yonks by publishers and authors seeking interviews on my little wireless program. Sadly I now know that they're of virtually no financial value, that no one wants them. So on my death they're destined for landfill. Fortunately they're biodegradable.

The End.

Aphorisms

While the world obsesses over the rhythms of algorithms I prefer the dance of aphorisms. Deriving from the Greek 'aphorismos' or late Latin 'aphorismus' they are brief, brilliant and often witty condensations of wisdom, the haiku of philosophy. A bit like proverbs.

Before revealing my two all-time favourites some common-and-garden examples of pithy perception. He who hesitates is lost. Easy come, easy go. Tis better to have loved and lost than never to have loved at all. A penny saved is a penny earned. All that glitters is not gold. Absence makes the heart go fonder. Lie down with dogs, get up with fleas. Absence makes the heart grow fonder. Live by the sword, die by the sword. It is better to be alone than in bad company. Don't judge a book by its cover. Curiosity killed the cat. Practise what you preach.

Oscar Wilde was the maestro of the form. A few amongst hundreds? The mystery of love is greater than the mystery of death. Questions are never indiscreet: answers sometimes are. The only thing one knows about human nature is that it changes. A man who does not think for himself does not think at all. Anyone can sympathise with the sufferings of a friend, but it takes a very fine nature to sympathise with a friend's success. He who stands most remote from his age is he who mirrors it best. There is only one thing worse than being talked about, and that is not being talked about.

American polymath Benjamin Franklin was pretty good at aphorisms too. Beware of little expenses; a small leak will sink a big ship. Beware of the young doctor and the old barber. Fish and visitors smell in three days. Keep your eyes wide open before marriage, half shut afterwards. Life's tragedy is that we get old too soon and wise too late.

Three men may keep a secret if two of them are dead.

My favourites? On his 80th-something birthday the great and oft-heroic cellist Pablo Casals held a press conference in Madrid. As we old blokes do Pablo was banging on about the sorry state of things when he stopped, paused and uttered two sentences that don't seem to fit. And yet, to this fellow octogenarian, they seem perfect.

'The situation is hopeless.' A beat. 'We must take the next step.' It seems universally applicable – to everything from war to racism and climate change.

And talking of climate change, I first heard my other favourite aphorism when I was chair of the Commission for the Future, established by Barry Jones, Hawke's minister for science. The CFF would soon bring the issue of the Greenhouse Effect, and global warming, to public attention but at that first meeting what I best remember is the following statement to the board by a UK scientist: 'Data isn't information. Information isn't knowledge. Knowledge isn't wisdom.'

We're drowning in data. Powerful people and organisations fight to gather and possess it. But in and of itself data is worthless. Like iron-ore it has to be processed – value-added until it becomes information. That too needs further refinement – into ingots of knowledge. Even then it's valueless – until and unless it becomes, yes, wisdom. Which seems more magical than the alchemical dream of turning base metal into gold.

It's all too apparent that there's not a lot of wisdom around. You could say the situation is hopeless. We must take the next step.

Happiness

Happiness, or the pursuit thereof, is enshrined in that most august of documents, the US Constitution, along with the right to bear arms. To a distant observer the latter seems to have been achieve with bells on whilst the former is as elusive as the pot of gold allegedly located at the end of Judy Garland's rainbow. Particularly if you happen to be black.

No mention is made of happiness in our duller version, so perhaps it's time to add it, along with constitutional recognition of the First Nations.

Americans pursue happiness in a vigorous variety of ways. Some find it in the possession of the weapons, (up to and including, it would seem, cruise missiles) they see as officially promised if not mandated. Others find happiness in sex, children, Pentecostal pursuits or via drugs or shopping – that other opiate of the people. There is also that vast entertainment – industrial complex of movies, streaming services, ultraviolent video games. It seems the cup runneth over, yet enough unhappiness survives to power the Trump vote and his treasonous attack on the Capitol.

In Australia we briefly attain a hint of happiness by voting out an unpopular government to make way for another doomed to become unpopular. We also shop til we drop, though this becomes difficult during high inflation when a strange melancholia sets in, except amongst the imperviously wealthy whose self-indulgences on posh products have helped Bernard Arnault replace Elon Musk as the world's richest person. Apparently Monsieur Arnault's contribution to civilization, at least the civilisation of the 1%, is to provide them with handbags and the sweet smell of success in the form of the fug of stratospherically expensive perfumes.

What do the sages o'er the ages have to say about happiness? Albert Einstein sounded quite Buddhist when recommending 'a calm and modest life rather than the pursuit of success combined with a constant restlessness'. Buddha himself said, 'There is no path to happiness: happiness is the path.' His current incarnation the Dalai Lama agrees. 'Happiness is not something readymade – it comes from you own actions.' Moved Dali, seconded Eleanor Roosevelt: 'Happiness is not a goal. It's a by-product of a life well-lived.' Carried on the voices, Voltaire said, probably in French, that, 'I have chosen to be happy because it's good for my health.' Gabriel Garcia Marquez concurred. 'No medicine can cure what happiness cannot.' I concur with Charles M. Schultz, author of *Peanuts*, who believed that, 'Happiness is a warm puppy.' Or presumably a kitten if you're not a dog person.

Grumpy old Mark Twain could not be cajoled. 'Sanity and happiness are an impossible combination.' But In a mellower mood Mr. Clemens advised that, 'the best way to cheer yourself up is to cheer someone else up.' Ralph Waldo Emerson? "For every minute you are angry you lose sixty seconds of happiness."

(Of course Ralph got a head start by having the witty middle name of Waldo, whereas I was cursed at the Rev. Adams' font with, shudder, Hedley).

One of my favourites comes from the Mahatma. Ghandi took time off from guiding India to guide us thus. 'Happiness is when what you think, what you say and what you do are in harmony.'

You may believe that's a waste of effort and opt for taking happy pills. Or go to the Giggle Palace at Luna Park. To each her own. Currently I've got a warm puppy.

Paper Papers

For years we've been told that the paper paper is heading for the exit. That the physical newspaper is as doomed as the Dodo or dinosaur. And to dramatise the point many readers are currently looking at a screen rather than a paper page. Though a subscriber to the digital edition I still insist on hard copy for the *Weekend Oz*. And it's not just out of sentiment, though that is certainly a factor.

My first job in media, 70 years ago, was as a paperboy. A paper paperboy. I dragged a billycart loaded with *Melbourne Sun*s and *Age*s from the local News Agency through the streets of East Melbourne, tossing 'orders' with gross inaccuracy at the front doors of terraces – or in the general direction of 'flats', as apartments were known. In wet weather the papers were sodden messes of mache.

At night I'd load the billycart with *Herald*s and head for my corner possie, where in return for the gross underpayment of five-pence a dozen, I'd dart between cars and jump on and off moving trams. Talk about child labour. It was as dangerous as being sent down a coal mine or up a chimney. Impossible to believe in these days of OHS.

Now many a masthead has been lowered to half-mast. Most of the papers and magazines I wrote for in later years are long gone. From the *Communist Guardian* (not to be confused with the surviving paper of the same name) to the conservative *Bulletin*. Goodbye *Nation*, *Nation Review* and the *National Times* wherein I once had by-lines. Others linger on in digital form, in a world where soon AI will be writing the stories and columns. Is *Time* still around? *Newsweek*? The *Readers Digest*?

Paper papers were recycled long before formal, fashionable recycling. Not for nothing were newspapers known as fishwraps. Fish 'n chip depended on them. And they often served as toilet paper in outside dunnies, torn into pieces and hung from a rusty nail. They also were used to line drawers or for the bottom of birdcages. On the farm newspapers were used as mulch for crops. Try any of the foregoing with your digital edition.

I knew a newspaper hoarder who piled them up with the intention of revisiting them at some point. He never did. Teetering, tottering towers of Melbourne *Herald*s, *Sun*s, *Argus* and *Ages* for the ages. And yes, a heavenly haven for rodents.

Now to the sentimentality factor. Apart from my early labours in the selling and delivery thereof I actually LIKE paper papers. I like their heft, even their smell. It's much the same with books. Give me a real one any day, limp or stiff as naughty Dame Edna calls them, rather than something digitised on a Kindle, whatever that is. Although I make an exception for the halfway house of the audiobook I use to dull the boredom of my 600 km commute.

Newspapers. It's an employment issue. OK, paperboys are no longer a factor. But without paper papers there's be no need to 'stop the presses'. No presses to start. And newsagents? Not lots to sell except lotto tickets.

I'm told kids don't read the news – either on paper or screen – that they get what little they know about the world from some Chinese plot called Tik Tok, not to be confused with the stop watch on *Sixty Minutes*.

Tick tock. Time is running out...

Isms

For much if its modern history the world has been defined and divided by -isms and -ologies. Theologies, ideologies – there's two of the biggest -oligies for you. Also on display in economic theories and the sciences. Ditto the pseudo-sciences. Think parapsychology versus psychology.

A random collection of -isms. Racism. Fascism. Nazism. Collectivism. Marxism – and sub-categories like Leninism and Stalinism. Poor Khrushchev and Gorbachev. Neither Nikita nor Mikhael made the ism cut. Nor were their bodies embalmed and entombed in Red Square.

You can add an -ism to just about anything that takes your fancy or raises ire or eyebrows – from baptism to cannibalism. But isms works best for beliefs and doctrines. Ask Karl, Hitler and Musso. With Donald Trumpism a recent addition.

(Fugitive thought. Will Donald be entombed in DC? Yes, of course after his death. In a gilded Trump Tomb in front of the Capitol? So he can storm it forever? Or he might prefer to be buried on one of his golf courses for tax purposes – as he did with an ex-wife)

And here's a truism. The greatest fights are not between political parties but within them. Look at the way factionalism has effed the ALP forever. Not the Libs though. You will remember Malcolm Turnbull saying 'there is no factionalism in the Liberal Party'. Given the response even he had to laugh.

Denialism has a long dark history. We've a history of denialism about the way we treated the First Nations people. Australia's own Eric Butler was, like David Irving, a Holocaust denier. The Vatican denied the paedophilia within the priesthood.

And when it comes to being a climate change deniers the queue forms on the right. And only on the Right. No climate denialists on the Left. Hi there Barnaby and the boys. Not to mention many of my journalism colleagues •

JournalISM. Just noticed that.

Fanaticism. Feminism. Sexism. Scepticism. Egoism. Ageism. Pentecostalism. Let's not forget differenceism – a dislike of anyone different. Mind you, there are a few nice ones. Optimism. Altruism. Pacifism. Humanism (count me in). Romanticism. Positivism.

Isms are huge when it comes to ideas in art. Realism. Mannerism. Dadaism. Impressionism. Fauvism. Pointillism. Surrealism. Cubism. Expressionism. Just slap your paint on in a different way, add an ism, and let the auction houses know.

Its much the same with ologies in medicine – think gastro, gyno, immun, cardio and, unfortunately, onc

I'm thinking of odder ologies. Astr-, Anthro-, Archae-. Paleont- Biol-, Ocean. Vampir-, Vulcanology, and watch the lava. Cosmo- and Astro are two of my favourites thanks to Carl Sagan. And geo- thanks to Simon Winchester.

We have the Ancient Greeks to thank for ologies – from as word meaning to talk, to speak. Ditto –ism. It's from another Greek word – meaning 'take sides with' or 'imitation of'. Think grand narrative.

I've been involved with many isms. Communism before the age of consent. That earned me an ASIO file at the age of 16. Very proud of that. Humanism came a little later – and was proud to be named Humanist of the Year by the Humanist Society, becoming one of the distinguished alumnus. And scepiticism is a life-long favourite – hence my modest involvement in establishing the Australian Sceptics

– in company with Dick Smith and fellow atheist Mark Plummer. I recommend their marvellous magazine *The Sceptical Enquirer*, home of the best debunkers.

As I prepare to exit the topic I recall the tautology and, as I rub my head, phrenology.

Petting

Humans have had pets since forever, probably starting with wolf pups in our cave days. Archaeological evidence dates petting and patting pets back over 30,000 years, probably beginning with the domesticating of wolf pups.

Since then dogs of every all shape and size – all descended from wolves – remain top of the pet pops. The last time I counted there were somewhere between 700,000 and a billion of them, all wanting to go walkies and chase balls.

Add to the menu or menagerie the pussy. Some people, for reasons I cannot fathom, prefer the descendants of sabre-tooth tigers. We are dividable between dog and cat people in much the same way as being Catholic or Protestant.

There are of course many other sorts of pets. There's that ratbag with his tiger – and the Manhattans with pet alligators that have escaped and now live in New York's sewers. A man in Alcatraz famously had pet birds, and many of us not encaged encage canaries and budgies. Although, oddly, Tony Abbott kept his budgie in his bathers.The biggest caged birds? Falconers into hunting train them all the way up to eagles. Illegal in Australia.

Snakes, tortoises, monkeys, lizards, white mice, various insects. – all can be pets. Prisoners other than that Alcatraz birdman have been known to have pet cockroaches. Fish from dolphins down to goldfish have their fans – and at age four I kept tadpoles in a jar. Trouble with taddies? They turn into frogs and abscond. I had more success with guinea pigs – and there's a story that Richard Gere had a pet gerbil.

Although far too intelligent to play cricket, Mandarin aristocrats kept pet crickets in exquisite boxes. I've a friend who collects them. The boxes, not the crickets. My biggest pet was a huge black bull I called Malcolm X. He came when I called – charging through any fences in his way. He liked to lift me aloft on his massive head. The missus and farm manager feared he'd kill me by accident and while I was in Sydney sold Malcolm to McDonalds. That well-intentioned betrayal almost made me a vegan. And I was tempted to convert from Humanism to Hinduism.

Some Japanese children had pet robots that looked like little dogs, but that seemed to me akin to making a pet out of mum's vacuum cleaner. Even less heart-warming? The Pet Rocks that made Gary Dahl a fortune. As he pointed out they didn't eat much or get sick or die. He sold thousands in the mid-seventies – in little cardboard kennels with ventilation holes.

Scott Morrison was this nation's most famous pet rocker. You'll remember him smuggling a pet lump of coal into parliament. It was beautifully coiffed and lacquered to prevent smudging Scomo's suit – though it did smudge his reputation. This was even more eccentric than Abbott smuggling his budgies.

(You'd have thought they'd have been diagnosed as insane but both became Prime Ministers. It was the voters who were nuts. An international problem. Think Trump, a bloke with even more rocks in his head, becoming President.)

Which bring us to us. Decades before AI a famous Australian scientist warned me that by interfering with slow-moving Darwinian evolution we might well invent super-humans or non-humans much smarter than ourselves, life forms that would make us redundant. Tossing ourselves into the dustbin of history.

As you know, that happened last Tuesday. I've never forgotten what he said next. 'Some of us might survive.'

'As pets.'

Ignorant

'Tis said that wisdom comes with age. 'Tis sad that's not the case in my case. As I head for the exit it's my glum duty to confess my ignorance of everything from A to Z. From astronomy to zoology. From accountancy to Zoroastrianism.

I'm wise in only one sense – when wisdom is defined as knowing what you don't know. Then I'm Einsteinian, a Renaissance Man – even though I know I cannot comprehend Einstein (WTF could E equals MC squared possibly mean?) and know SFA about the Renaissance.

Some of my ignorance can be blamed on a state school education – not its quality but its brevity. East Kew Primary, Yarra Park State and Eltham High did their best. But I was a poor student and left the system at the under-ripe young age of 15. As I once observed the nearest I got to university was once passing Melbourne Uni on the Lygon Street tram.

There's a posh term for the likes of me. Autodidact. But just as I missed the tertiary tram (as opposed to that one in Lygon Street), I failed to catch the auto. So what little I've learned came from books (three cheers for public libraries) and the university of life. From which I'll soon be expelled. (An admission: Six universities have taken pity and given me funny gowns and silly hats. These are otherwise known as Honorary Doctorates, so I'm technically Dr Dr Dr Dr Dr Dr Adams. It's their way of thanking me for interviewing all their actual graduates, that endless procession of professors).

Among the subjects of which I'm utterly ignorant is sport. This is wilful on my part. I regard sport as loud, aggressive and likely to cause injury. Ditto all forms of popular music since the deaths of Bing Crosby and Bill Haley. Same reason as sport: loud aggressive and likely to cause injury, in this latter case deafness.

The other reason I know next to nothing? There's too much to know. And humans are forever adding new things to know and I find that both intimidating and dispiriting. So what's the point? Leave knowing stuff to the professional know-alls, all those professors I interview.

Or look it up on Wikipedia, that satnav for members of DENSA, my parallel MENSA for dills. What does it matter what I know or don't know as long as somebody knows it?

Speaking of dills I can't even answer the low-IQ multiple-choice questions on *Millionaire Hotseat*. And as for knowing all about some utterly obscure topic on *Mastermind,* count me out. I remember a bloke answering lots of questions about *Don's Party* that I couldn't – and I produced the bloody movie!

And speaking of television I don't understand who did it in an episode of *Poirot* even when Hercule has explained it. Yes, that could be a symptom of my dementia.

Ignorance is bliss? BS. What a silly assertion for some ignoramus to make. My ignorance is not blissful. It would be bliss not to be ignorant. But it's too late now.

Or it is? Perhaps I could get a chat-bot to write a grovelling letter to Eltham High and see if they'd let me sneak back in. As a mature-age student. To belatedly earn my Leaving Certificate. And if not, perhaps the school Principal might take pity on me – and given me an honorary one. Wouldn't even expect another funny hat.

Tortoise

Today, what the tortoise has taught us.

Were I to say Aeschylus you might say 'bless you!' thinking I'd sneezed rather than drawing your attention to the Ancient Greek who had top billing in local theatre as 'the father of tragedy'.

He wrote about 90 of them, of which, tragically, few survive. We know his name better because of the way he died, not so much a tragedy as a farce. By being hit on his head by a tortoise. Crowned if you will, by a combination of its carapace and the force of gravity. Little gravitas for Aeschylus – the only human in history to die in such an improbable manner.

It sees an eagle had lifted the creature high aloft and was looking for a hard rock to drop it on, so as to gain access to the contents of the carapace when it mistook the playwright's bald head for a small boulder. And the rest is history.

As I write these woeful words at the farm I can see a pair of wedge-tails circling in a thermal so will remember to take care. You may well laugh but an eagle once swooped down and grabbed our Jack Russell, dropping it only when realising it was too weighty. No damage, only to the dog's dignity. As I was chasing the raptor at a time Willy might well have landed on my balding noggin and I'd have gone down – and down in history too. What Spike Milligan described as 'the dreaded deadings' – by a flying terrier.

Tortoises are rarely into aviation. They leave that to Mr Joyce's kangaroo. So notoriously earthbound (i.e. we not paddling the water) that Aesop used co-stars to feature in a fable about a tortoise racing a hare. Spoiler alert: the tortoise won, though stewards are demanding a swab.

Tortoises can often be found trying to cross the Gundy Road in search of sex in the local river or adjacent dams. Some vile humans try and run over them. Daughter Rory and I were forever saving them – popping them in the boot for re-housing them in one of Elmswood's dams or fishponds. But be warned. Tortoise pee is pungent. Compared to your typical skunk it's as fragrant as a flower.

Their big siblings the turtles have legendarily long lifespans, as those on Galapagos and elsewhere attest. They can also be enormous – such heavyweights that I remember riding on one as a child. Back in the days when you were also encouraged to ride elephants at zoos. They also look large in mythology

There was an ancient belief that our world was held on the back of a giant turtle. When a sceptic asked WTF held up the turtle he was told 'another turtle... and another beneath that. It's turtles all the way down'.

From myths to movies. Remember the 'Ninja Turtles'? I don't but someone mentioned them. Perhaps they're related to the Mock Turtles of soup fame.

In boom times, between droughts, our dams brim with them. You see them traffic-jammed. Then off they go. Just as the grass is always greener the waters always wetter. In search of love you see them bravely trudging along dusty tracks – not in a race against any hares but dehydration. A race against time. Often they lose, and you see the sad sight of a dried-out shell.

Yep, in the farm's vast menagerie of wild things the 'tortie' is our favourite.

Qantas

Dear Ms Hudson

May I call you Vanessa? I write to congratulate you on taking over what's left of Qantas from the Lethal Leprechaun (my not–very-pet-name for Alan) with a few suggestions that might be of interest.

Firstly, renationalise the airline. This patriotic proposition is already gaining momentum from those who remember Qantas in its halcyon days. I'm one of them and have, as they say, skin in the game. Forty-odd years ago I presented my marketing credentials to the board when your role was filled by the popular John 'Tubby' Ward and, as I recall, Jim Leslie was Chair.

Qantas' mercy fights from a cyclone ravaged Darwin were still fresh in the memory. Yes, Qantas was truly the national carrier – of many hundreds of refugees. It was a time when, around the world, returning Aussies would be greeted by cabin crew with a friendly grin – and 'G'day, welcome on board'. No matter where you were you were already half way home

It wasn't just the perfect safety record that made us proud of the world's second-oldest airline (only the Dutch KLM was older). It was the Qantas ethos, 'the vibe' if you like.

Hence my suggestion to the board of a new motto. I can still see the smiles as I unveiled it. THE SPIRIT OF AUSTRALIA. It soon appeared on everything from aircraft fuselages to boarding passes to the paper serviettes provided with the little bowl of peanuts. I subsequently suggested Qantas acquire Peter Allen's anthem *I Still Call Australia Home*. Two perfect fits.

The downward spiral began, as with so many Australian institutions, with privatisation and accelerated with the Leprechaun. Alan found many pots of gold for himself at the end if the airline's rainbow but others weren't so lucky. Not the pilots, not the cabin crews, not the ground crews, not the engineers – and certainly not the passengers. Or customers as they were to be known.

Using Covid as camouflage, savage staffing cuts were made, engineering went off shore, the safety record was compromised, the fleet became old to the point of arthritic. As I publicly complained countless times the airline did NOT call Australia home – and did NOT deserve my motto. Qantas was NOT the Spirit of Australia.

In recent times a dispirited mockery of the Spirit of Australia has wreaked such havoc on the company's reputation that all the 'loyalty programs' on earth will no longer restore the loyalty of passengers once loyal without the dubious inducements of FFPs. And the final departure of Alan Joyce will not be of national mourning.

Much is expected of you Vanessa, or at least hoped. But the task!!

Soon, like Elvis, Alan will have left the building. With his usual inability to read the room his final decision seems to have been an apologetic phone call to Alan Jones. Mr. Jones had just learnt of his eviction from that most inner of sanctums, the Chairman's Lounge.

Vanessa, your Mission Near Impossible, should you agree to accept it, is not to placate a shocked jock about the Chairman's Lounge but to rebuild the lost trust of your staff and your passengers – so that once again Qantas can call Australia home – and be deserving of my motto. I'll check back with you in a few months.

This message will self-destruct in ten seconds.

Yours most sincerely,

Phillip

Honest John

All of us, every human being irrespective of colour, religion or postcode, are 99.9% identical. DNA's double helix makes it clear that you, King Charles, Donald Trump and Mark Latham, to choose a few humans at random, are separated by just 0.1%. Thanks heavens for that 0.1%.

But some of us are even closer. Me and John Howard for example. Despite some subtle political differences we're peas in a pod. Born just hours apart in July 1939 we've become grumpy old buggers, bald and hard of hearing, who having run out of relevance are heading for the exit. John is no longer the Libs' secret weapon – recent interventions in elections haven't helped their vote. For the young? He's John Whoward.

Both of us shared a repugnance for retirement. His was forced upon him by mutinous voters, mine approaches via poor health. Yet oddly I've John to thank for the length of my innings. As PM he was asked to define what was wrong with the ABC. His response? 'Where's the right-wing Phillip Adams?'

Fun fact. I've never been an ABC staffer, relying on 30-odd annual contracts. And make no mistake – there have been many attempts to evict me from the premises – another earlier this year. John's useful question gave me job security, albeit briefly, for the first and last time. And in desperate attempts to balance my bias the ABC had to hire a succession of right wing mes, including Tim Blair, Tom Switzer and Amanda Vanstone.

John and I belong to a mutual detestation society. He sees me as a pimple on the bum of the body politics, I see him (against stiff competition) as our worst-ever Prime Minister.

Although the blame for much of his dark history might rest on spouse Jeanette, effectively our first female PM. Based on the eye-witness accounts of John Hewson you'll find the lurid details in my indispensable *Backstage Politics* (Penguin).

Time to confess that I've slept with Jeanette on three occasions – when some Qantas larrikin gazumped my preferred seat – 1A – and gave it to Mrs. Howard, plonking me in 1B. Ever the gentleman and seeing her pained expression I'd soothingly say 'Not to worry, I'm passing out' and would. But I couldn't resist the temptation to reveal our intimate sleeping arrangements on air.

Why our worst PM? We have Honest John to thank for the horrors of Hansonism, for the endless cruelty of our refugee policy – and for our involvement in the invasion of Iraq. Bob Woodward, the ultimate US insider, told me that Howard didn't just 'go along' with George W in the Coalition of the Willing but 'greatly influenced' a wavering President. One of the most fateful, fatal farces in the history of foreign policy (sic) continue as a consequence of this catastrophic decision – with millions murdered maimed, maddened and displaced.

In this context Howard's gun laws after Port Arthur don't cut it. In any case, as Paul Keating told me at the time, no PM would have had any choice.

Add it all up, and there's a lot to add, my nomination of Howard as worst-ever PM is as defensible as his term in office wasn't. Others have been foolish or incompetent – McMahon, Abbott, Turnbull and Morrison come to mind – but they're bronze, silver and lead medallists compared to Howard's gold.

So John, happy birthday to you. And, while I'm at it, to me. 84 and counting.

In a Jam

It was a time of danger. Of letter bombs, of envelopes containing anthrax, of paranoia about parcels. One of which arrived at my Sydney home that my secretary Sandra deemed suspicious. I was at the ABC that morning and, showing her usual enterprise, Sandra tossed the parcel – a very heavy one – into the swimming pool.

Later I fished it out, peeled off the soggy brown paper and gingerly opened the flaps... to reveal a dozen jars of marmalade, an annual gift from a reader named Simonette. When I told her what had happened to her jam she said 'I won't make that mistake again'. And as you are about to learn, she didn't.

(Sandra was right to be cautious. Only a few weeks earlier a reader, infuriated by a column, had posted me a turd. Australia Post had delivered it – gladwrapped in a jiffy bag – in mint condition).

Flash-forward a year. Another parcel arrives for me – at the ABC HQ in Ultimo. Where it immediately arouses suspicion in the mail room.

It's not that it's menacingly ticking anything but an alert staffer thinks my name is written 'in lettering that looks a bit Islamic'.

Immediately alarms are sounded and the entire building is evacuated. All the TV and radio studios, all the executive offices, backstage areas, the cafeteria and the car park. Sleeping babies in the ABC crèche are carried to safety. Hundreds of bewildered people are mustered gather outside into Harris St.

(Knowing nothing of this I'm in my office at home with Sandra answering run-of-the-mill hate mail).

The cops are notified and the ABC awaits the arrival of the Bomb Squad, expecting armoured vehicles containing, at very least, sniffer dogs and men waddling in heavy protective clothing. We know what to expect from TV dramas – the deployment of a remote-controlled robot that will approach the parcel, prod it with a metal nose and probably shoot it full of holes.

But this is Australia.

Instead a couple of young cops from the local Police Station arrive in a Falcon, casually toss the parcel in the boot and drive off. No drama, no fuss, no worries. With a collective sigh of relief the staff troop back to their tasks in TV, radio and management. And the babies are returned to the crèche. What passes for peace is restored. The incident will not even rate that night's news.

Finally Sandra gets call from the ABC to inform me of what's happened. It was, after all, my parcel, my fault.

Immediately I'm suspicious. Could it possibly be that this year Simonette, to avoid Sandra and the swimming pool, sent my marmalade to the ABC? I make tentative enquiries. Finally the police confirm the fact that, yes, the mysterious parcel contained a dozen jars of marmalade.

In coming weeks all is explained to Simonette and Sandra is tasked with the task of getting my jam out of a jam. Indeed out of jail. But this never happens. It is still mouldering away in an evidence locker? Or did the happy-go-lucky kids in the Falcon share the loot back at the cop shop? I like to think the latter as I reckon they deserved it. No hint of corruption here – just an appropriate reward for Australian-style heroism.

It'd make a great plot for a Law and Order Oz. The show with the ding ding. Remind me to email this column to Dick Wolf.

Super

Superman. Batman. Ironman. Spiderman. Antman. And the token Wonder Woman. A vast menagerie of superannuated superheros, all ultra-American, all fascistic, all running around in their Technicolor underwear.

And talking of fascist tendencies I understand that DC Comics will launch TrumpMan in time for the next presidential elections.

The usual gross overload of Captain American heroes. Coca-Colonisation at its worst. Not an Australian amongst them. For some reason Ben Roberts-Smith has been shelved – from superhero to zero. But where's Kelly Man (Ned Man?) the original iron man in his trusty rusty undies? All those sissy masked heroes flying around in in pretty fabrics would be in awe. Call that a mask? THIS is a mask. Ned's cozzie, metal from noggin to groin. OK, history reminds us that his armour wasn't 100% bullet-proof, but the best superstars have their poignant vulnerabilities. Remember kryptonite? But no one has bettered our iron man's ironic exit line. 'Such is life.'

To hell with Superman. We want Swagman, Australia's Creature From the Black Billabong. Ready to leap old shearing sheds in a single kangaroo-inspired bound – with his rallying cry of 'Waltzing Matilda' (Fugitive thought: where does Clark Kent change into his undies now that the smart phones have retired the phone-booth?) Making matters worse any number of Australian thespians rushed off to play US superheroes – Eric Bana, Sam Worthington and Hugh Jackman.

To correct this cultural cringe I hereby announce the first dozen denizens of my down-under-fair-dinkum world of southern-hemispherical-heroes.

Bugger off Batman, lurking in your bat cave beneath Gotham City, waiting to be summoned by a bat signal projected via searchlight. Welcome to his antipodean alter-ego …the wonderful Wombat-Man!! Living in his secret burrow up the back paddock. (When you want him just borrow the spotlight off a local rabbit hunter). Not as bat-like as the womBAT name suggests he mightn't be much chop at flying, but boy-oh-boy he'll come down very heavily on any miscreant. The Joker'll run a mile or, splat! be squashed flat.

I'm warming to Wombat Man. Not as showy as some. But he could burrow beneath tall buildings. And what about Bullant Man to beat AntMan? And a Wombat Woman for gender balance. I once christened Billy Kelty the Killer Koala – that physical resemblance. Koala a Man? There might be something there. Your suggestions welcome. (Which reminds me. Superheroes need super villians. Do let's swap the Joker for our Laughing Jackass). Looking around for other supermen I'm tempted to recruit Barry Jones, Gough and Paul Keating. And HawkeMan (BobMan?) has an avian, somewhat batty, ring to it.

But I mentioned the fascistic overtones of the superheroic earlier. So perhaps we should look at our right-wing pollies. Tony Abbott's famous budgie smugglers provide a ready-to-wear cozzie – while the ScoMo name has a near anagramic comic-book ring to it. And if you want evidence of superhuman strength look at all his simultaneously held ministries. Not even a combination Captain Marvel and Mighty Mouse could match that. And to avoid accusations of political bias I'm thinking of Barnaby Man. Remember how Popeye the Sailorman gained great strength by downing a can of spinach? I envisage Barnaby getting his by drinking a few tinnies. We could call him Beetroot Man

BradMan? The Don's an off-the-shelf idea. Kanga Man? Yabbie Man – our Aqua Man? Don't hold back. And who says we have to stay boringly binary?

My Way

It was not the fault of the Frenchman who wrote the original song 'Comme d'habitude' Blame it on Canadian Paul Anka. In 1967 he wrote American lyrics for a French song that had nothing to do with death – and it became a huge hit for Frank Sinatra. *My Way*.

Soon it was as familiar at funerals as the *Wedding March* at nuptials. I'm not sure if they played it at Frank's but it seems to have been inflicted on mourners at everyone else's.

Anka's words were, to put in kindly, pretty abysmal. 'I did what I had to do and saw it through without exemption'. The unmusical sounds you hear are Cole Porter, Ira Gershwin, Noel Coward, Irving Berlin and Oscar Hammerstein moaning in their graves. They did it their way so much better than Anka did his.

But I liked the opening gambit. 'And now the end is near – and so I face the final curtain'. Verily I say unto you beloved readers that we're all heading to that fatal fabric at the same inexorable pace, but some of us, particularly my fellow octogenarians, will arrive somewhat sooner. And I'm damned sure I won't be having Sinatra sing *My Way* at my exit. I'd prefer something less self-aggrandising and more cheerful. Suggestions welcome.

The Sinatra/Anka dirge is not the only glum song to be sung at rites of passage. Take *Happy Birthday*, as much fun as the *Death March*. Dishwater-dull words to a tuneless tune. The birthday cake with its effing candles only adds to the gloom. And the victim of this cruel and callous ceremony is expected to happily blow the damn things out. Huffing and puffing to extinguish your years.

And at my age all those candles threaten to set off the smoke alarms

– or break the regulations during bushfire season.

Even the aforementioned *Wedding March* has an ominous sound to it. Bride and groom to their marital doom. Apparently young Felix Mendelsohn wrote it for a production of Shakespeare's *Midsummer Night's Dream*. Given the accelerating failure rate of marriages – even more numerous than *Midsomer Murders* – there's clearly an opportunity for a latter-day Felix to belt out a *Divorce March*. There goes the bride.

But back to Mr. Anka. Some of his words pass muster. "I've lived a life that's full – I've travelled each and every highway" isn't too dusty – but then he loses it entirely with "there were times I'm sure you knew when I bit off more than I can chew" which gets even more disgusting with "I ate it up and spit it out". Regurgitate rhyming to give you reflux.

Anka's attempts at philosophising are more chunderous and sink like an anchor. "For what is man, what has he got? If not himself then he has naught." More deep moanings from Cole, Ira, Irving, Oscar and Noel. Let alone Stevie Sondheim.

Regrets? Frank had a few –'but then too few to mention'. This suggests repressed memories or moral dementia. Dunno about you, but I've got countless regrets – a myriad examples of commission and omission. I could spend weeks made up of personal sorry days.

What brought all this on? Written whilst awaiting what's euphemistically known as a 'surgical procedure'. As Samuel Johnson observed when musing on mortality 'Be sure of it, Sir. When a man knows he is to be hung in a fortnight it concentrates the mind wonderfully'.

The Gunited States

Too many nations have blood-soaked histories. Hitler's Germany – Stalingrad, Leningrad and the Holocaust. Stalin's Soviet with the Gulags, Belgium with Leopold's butchery of millions in the Congo. The colonial cruelties perpetrated by Spain, France, Britain. Japanese atrocities like the Rape of Nanking. China's Cultural Revolution and its tyranny in Tibet. Israel with the Palestinians. Apartheid South Africa. Australia with our poisonings, massacres and enslavement of First Nations peoples. Our treatment of refugees.

But the nation with the deepest and most pervasive culture of violence? The Gunited States of America.

Since its birth in the War of Independence the US has had hardly a year of peace. Even before Eisenhower's warning of the 'Military Industrial Complex' it fought scores of wars across the planet. And always seems to yearn for more – all too often on the wrong side of history. This is before you count in the covert wars that, for example, resulted in the 9/11 of Chile. Or the CIA's ludicrous attempts to kill Castro with poisoned cigars. Or to assassinate Julian Assange.

Almost a million die in the Civil War. Countless more in wars against Mexico and the so-called Indian Wars, those genocidal attacks on Native Americans. And continuing to drive US history – the monstrous violence of the transatlantic slave trade and the home-grown slave economy. For decades lynch mobs would hang African Americans by the thousand – to the applause of happy crowds of white men, women and children. Lynchings were as popular as State Fairs. As Billy Holiday sang 'Southend trees bear strange fruit, blood on the leaves and blood at the root'. And still they continue in the legal judicial system.

Long before Trump's Proud Boys' insurrection at the Capitol the KKK (ten million members at its peak – murdered countless blacks – and their white supporters – during the second Civil War of the Civil Rights Movement. And never forget the on-going police killings that provoked Black Lives Matter.

The US incarcerates a higher percentage of its population than any other nation – and remains one of the most enthusiastic employers of the death penalty. Once again with a disproportionate percentage of blacks.

Armed militias of white supremicists engage in domestic terror – adding to the efforts of Unabombers and Oklahoma City Bombers. Martin Luther King Jr, Malcolm X and Bobby Kennedy are assassinated – along with US presidents. And for every successful killing of a president there are a score of attempts.

Serial killers abound and have fan clubs. Massacres in schools have become a tradition – thanks to grotesque or non-existent gun laws. Having learned nothing from the gangsterism of Prohibition, the long-lost Drug War, gang wars rage in the ghettos – and suburbs burn from Watts to LA. Killing is celebrated in cinema and television. The echoes of dystopian fantasies are deafening. Remember how GWB's shock-and-awe attack on Iraq reminded us of video games?

And the US remains the only nation to have used nuclear weapons, dropped not one but two A-bombs in one of history's greatest war crimes.

With as many handguns as hands, Americans shoot their fellow citizens on a daily basis while that military industrial complex makes it the world's largest exporter of weaponry. And it is home to a criminal ex-President who orchestrated an armed coup against his own country – yet who may well, despite impeachments and injunctions, gain a second term.

Scouts

I must be one of the few Australians to have been expelled from both the Communist Party and the Boy Scouts, though not in that order. Having joined the former shortly after being booted from the latter. From post-Stalin Bolshevism to Baden-Powell's 'broomstick warriors'.

Bolshevism first. Having joined the Australian Communist Party at 15 (bemused comrades at the Eltham branch waived the usual minimum-age requirements) it's debatable whether I was pushed or jumped. The Party was simultaneously im/exploding and if you were a rat jumping ship you were evicted.

Perhaps it's in my ASIO file. I'm proud that I was the youngest to have one! Having finally got it from the National Archives, albeit heavily redacted, it's one of my proudest possessions.

But today it's my drum-head court martial from the Scouts, one of the greatest miscarriages of justice since the Dreyfus Case or the defeat of Scott Morrison.

I'd been a Cub at East Kew, but after moving to East Melbourne joined a troop that met in the basement of a bluestone Anglican Church in that more gentrified suburb. There I learned to tie knots – difficult for a left-hander – while chanting 'DYB' or 'Do your best', one of the many Lodge-like rituals demanded by the Scouting's imperialistic military founder Baden-Powell. The organisation was made up of Brownies and Guides (girls) and Cubs, Scouts and Rangers (boys).

My night of the long knives (broomsticks?) occurred when fellow Scouts were sneaking a furtive fag (as I recall, sharing a packed of Turf) when we heard the dreaded tread of the Scout Master coming down the stairs. Obedient to the Scouting motto of 'Be Prepared' I rounded up the smouldering evidence and shoved the butts into a desk drawer. Then, during inspection, when the SM was checking our woggles (Google the term for details) the papers in the drawer caught fire and ignited the desk.

Who was responsible for this conflagration? Although the packet of Turf had been stolen from his father by Arthur Hodges he pointed the finger at moi. No brave chorus of 'I'm Spartacus' from the other pubescent gladiators. I was arrested, charged, denied legal representation and found guilty. Forced to hand over woggle and broomstick and leave the basement. Cast into outer darkness and eternal ignominy. Now, 70 years later, I'm thinking of suing for libel, slander, defamation and damages while demanding the return of my woggle.

Did the Scouting movement survive? Are there still boys and girl Cubs, Scouts and Rangers (I hope so, for who else will teach kids knots)? Is there still a troop in the church basement? Is there still a Chief Scout – descended from Baron Baden-Powell from whom I can demand a belated apology?

I recall something about the US Scouts filing for bankruptcy following allegations of rampant paedophilia second only to the Vatican's. I saw no evidence of that at East Melbourne, but I must ask my betrayer Hodges. Still around Arthur?

But even without sexual shenanigans you can see, beloved readers, that I've suffered long term psychological damage – and have been unable to remain long in any organisation since. I usually attribute my leaving the Commos to ideology or my more recent resignation from the ALP to the coup against comrade Kevin. But I now blame the Scouts. Yes I've been at the ABC for 35 years but feel another premature resignation coming on.

Malcolm X

Over our 40 years we've had a plethora or pets. Horses, big and little, a herd of donkeys, sheep, an alpaca we called Kerry, a joey that peed all over Paul Keating's Zegna suit, an aggressive turkey, pulchritudinous peacocks – both polychromatic and a pure white – all killed by foxes, a dozen dogs mostly destined to die of snakebite and, unbeknownst to us, an indoor snake that lived beneath a telly set for years, as evidenced by the shed shimmery skins it left behind. Just where baby Rory learned to crawl.

But the pet that loomed largest in the landscape was a bull. No ordinary bull but a whopper, a bull's bull – the big black Brahmin we called Malcolm. Not after Fraser or Turnbull but X, in honour of one of America's martyrs.

Over the years we've experimented with cattle breeds. English Herefords, some 'low-lines' (aka miniature cattle) and, given the area was founded by Scotch Presbyterians and with the nearest town being Aberdeen, Angus.

But as the droughts deepened we decided to try Brahmins, believed to be the best-adapted to dry conditions. So, one morning, we were gazing into a yard of pushing, shoving Brahmin bulls.

Some enchanted morning you may see a stranger across a crowded pen. And it's love at first sight. To borrow more from that Hammerstein lyric 'Who can explain it, who can tell you why? Fools give you reasons, wise men never try.'

I was instantly smitten. And it seemed, the feeling was mutual. We bonded forever. We were Romeo and Romeo – or Romoo-eo? God knows Malcolm had his choice of bovine beauties, Juliets jostling for his amorous attentions. I'd look for him after his day doing what bulls are born to do. If laying exhausted, I'd sit on him. If he was standing ruminating I'd come up and reward him with a piece of fruit. His response? He'd lift me aloft on his huge head.

When not in view I'd call him and he'd come trotting across a 1,000-acre paddock. But I had to be careful. If there was a fence between us he'd simply crash through it. Dragging the barbed-wires behind him like a necklace.

It became a party trick with visitors. I'd tell them about Malcolm and, in response to their disbelief, give them a demo. I'd call 'M-al-c-o-l-m!!' and then, after a few minutes, he'd arrive. And lift me up on his head.

This cordiality was not extended to others. Our bromance involved a one-man bull and a one-bull man. So it became of growing concern to the family and our farm manager, Phil Gilbert. There was a mounting fear that, inevitably, our friendship would end in grief. That quite by accident this gigantic creature would crush me.

So, one day after my usual week in Sydney, I returned to find no sign of Malcolm. There was no response to my calls. Enquiries led to blank expressions, feigned innocence.

Finally it became clear that Malcolm was no longer with us. Had he had a heart attack? Fallen off a cliff? Relentless interrogation led to the confession that he'd been sent to the sale yards and probably ended up in a few thousand Big Macs. It was almost enough to make me a vegetarian.

But Malcolm's ghost may be heard. Sometimes I feel that if I called he'd come thundering. Dragging a few fences behind him.

The A Bomb

Born a few weeks before the outbreak of WWII, I was six when the Enola Gay dropped the Atom Bomb on Hiroshima. A child of the atomic age, my nickname at East Kew Primary was Adam Bomb.

Talking to Robert Monk about his biography of J. Robert Oppenheimer my memories came rushing back. Including the memory of something Japan has preferred to forget. And wants the world to forget: the inconvenient truth that Japan, as well as the US and Germany, was working on the A Bomb. How do I know this? Because a bloke called Teddy Conant told me.

Here's the essence of the story. As a child Ted was bounced on Einstein's knee. His father, James B. Conant, held many senior positions in US academic, military and diplomatic life, including the Presidency of Harvard and as his country's first Ambassador to West Germany.

Having worked on the grim science of poison gas he would, years later, be placed in charge of the Manhattan Project – to build the bomb. He was one of the official dignitaries who witnessed the first Trinity detonation and a member of the committee that advised Truman to bomb Hiroshima. Later, from a change of heart, he would oppose the development of Teller's H Bomb.

Forty years ago Conant's son Teddy, who looked eerily like Jerry Lewis's nutty professor, was working for me – heading a team refining a unique Australian 3D system for film and television. Kerry Packer was our financier. We had R&D teams working in five cities.

We were flying to visit technicians in Tokyo when Teddy dropped the metaphoric bombshell – quite casually. That the Japanese were working on the bomb. I was incredulous, disbelieving. This was unknown to the wider world – and to those of us who regarded the US bombings as war crimes.

On our arrival Teddy introduced me to an ex-journalist friend now working in the communications satellite business. Previously he'd been researching, yes, Japan's secret nuclear program, a book that was never published. He played us wire recordings of interviews with Japanese scientists who confessed their involvement and that they hadn't been wildly successful. But nor, it emerged, were the Germans.

I heard him ask an ancient Japanese general the question. 'Would you have used it?' The answer was chilling in its simplicity. After a laugh, 'Of course!'

This changes nothing and everything.

Oppenheimer's team built three bombs for the Trinity project, each technically different. One for testing at Los Alamos, two for use. Critics of the decision to bomb Japanese cities argue: 1. that the bombs did not hasten the end of the war – that Japan as already defeated. 2. that the bomb would never have been used against a white enemy. 3. that the bomb should have been demonstrated to the world in the desert at Los Alamos rather than deployed. 4. that its real purpose was to frighten the USSR – to effectively declare the Cold War.

What seems clear to me is that the fact of a Japanese nuclear project at very least changes perception of Hiroshima and Nagasaki. Yet nobody knows about it. Least of all in modern Japan.

Those who did know are long dead. Including my friend Teddy. But it's part of the story of Oppenheimer, now being retold in the Nolan epic.

The nuclear club has eight sovereign members. The Doomsday Clock back at seconds to midnight… lest we forget.

Tree Hugging

Before turning Bernard Shaw's *Pygmalion* into *My Fair Lady* the US team of Lerner and Lowe wrote *Paint Your Wagon*. Set in Canada during the gold rush it contained a number of songs with odd titles – like *They Call the Wind Maria* and, proving my theme for today, *I Talk to the Trees.*

At the age of five I was on very intimate terms with a peppercorn tree at Grandpa's farm (a relationship I've written about in the past) I never actually spoke to it. Spike Milligan's version of the Lerner and Lowe song seems relevant here. 'I talk to the trees,' Spike warbled. 'That's why they put me away.'

Yet perhaps we should talk to trees, if only to express gratitude for their beauty, their shade, their timber, their important role in carbon capture. Or apologise to them for hacking them down in their billions (think of the Amazon basin) or letting them burn in the bushfires we intensify with climate change.

You may recall that our current king, when Prince of Wales, used to talk to pot-plants in the belief that this encouraged their growth. But they didn't put him away. It was seen as one of his charming eccentricities, like Camilla. And who knows? Perhaps it worked. Whether our newly minted monarch also talks to their larger rellos is unknown – perhaps he converses with the mighty oaks at Windsor or that mournful pile in Scotland. Sneaking out for a quiet, confidential chat when nobody's looking. If so, goodoh. Your average tree is probably as good a conversationalist as most homo sapiens.

The Greens don't take it far enough. I'm on record advocating that trees not only get the vote but be elected to parliament. I envisage local branches in leafy suburbs meeting to nominate candidates. No branch stacking.

And let us remember that tree-hugging has a long history. It was necessary for us whilst we lived in them prior to becoming bipedal. And more recently one great statesperson hugged trees all the time.

Fun fact. Otto Von Bismarck, that most prominent of Prussians, was known to adjourn meetings on weighty matters for the purposes of rejuvenation. He'd wander into the garden, select a suitable tree and embrace it warmly. No hint of eroticism – nothing kinky about our Otto. He just found that tree-hugging gave him the energy to resume the discussion on whatever. The future of Europe, or the German Reich or the need for a single currency.

Which is why I'm asking a leading intellect amongst the eucalypts to introduce a Private Member's Bill at the next session of our federal parliament. To have large trees planted around Parliament for all MP's and Senators to hug – is the confident belief it would improve the quality of government. And the same applies to both the High Court and Yarralumla. Our loftiest judges would obviously benefit in their deliberations – and the current Governor General clearly needs to hug a tree to make him more firmly rooted.

Before we're all rooted.

This column was written with the help of a surviving tract of Old Growth Forest – and I'd peculiarly like to thank a mighty Huon Pine who runs rings around any human I've encountered. Thanks to Bob Brown for the intro.

PS. I'm getting a new app for my iPhone – so I can make trunk calls.

Parky

There are many ways to conduct media interviews. They can be a ruthless interrogation, like a cross- examination in court or a coronial enquiry. They can be formal 'tick-the-box' pieces where the interviewer is effectively following a script. There's the stock-model puff piece. And Caroline Jones, in her *Search For Meaning* series on spiritual lives, used to emit little moans of pleasure – you felt like you were eavesdropping on a love scene. And there was Parky.

Long before we were required to keep up with the Kardashian humans we were celebrating celebrities. God, prophets, messiahs, sporting heroes, Lord Byrons and Oscar Wildes. But in this era of celebrity culture (sic) nobody did it better than Michael.

At a rough count I've interviewed almost 30,000 people. Anyone who can top than belongs in the *Guinness Book of Records*. Parky, in contrast, interviewed just 1,500 – but he went for quality rather than quality. Only the most celebrated celebs made the cut. And even then Parkie was picky.

Eschewing controversy Parky shunned any dangerous topics. Politics and religion we pitch. His shtick was showbiz. If interested in the big issues of the time you looked elsewhere.

Nor did he take risks with guests. His were professional interviewees – and only the most reliable showstoppers. Hence Dame Edna was a regular. And the show, though unrehearsed and unscripted, was close to a foregone conclusion. Guests were researched and pre-interviewed at length, primed to retell their best anecdotes, Michael's questions ready on his clipboard. To demonstrate this I recall a crisis when, returning to his seat after an encounter with a musical guest at a piano, Michael realised he'd forgotten to retrieve the clipboard. To signal his problem to his floor manager Michael said to the next guest, Britt Ekland, briefly the missus Peter Sellers: 'I don't know what to ask you.' Misinterpreting the moment the brick-thick Britt soothingly said, 'Just treat me like an ordinary person'.

In a backstage conversation with Sir Michael I suggested he make a slight change to his format. Yes, have your usual megastars as guests one and three, but use them as human bookends for a different number two – a non-celeb. Someone with something significant to say. Use your show to air an idea, an issue. Parky paled at the thought and changed the subject.

I was trying to make a useful, helpful point – based on personal experience. On many nights my show would issue an invitation to a novice who'd never been interviewed before and probably never would again – but someone that had that 'something important to say', often something surprising that deserved to be heard. Such ingénue guests would often prove to be the most memorable.

But if it ain't broke don't fix it. Michael had a winning formula that served him well for 500 shows. And of all the people who've interviewed me – and the tables have been turned many times over the decades – he was the most impeccably professional and charming. Against some stiff competition.

I've been interviewed by a bumptious John Singleton – 'Singo' had his own short-lived chat show – and the lofty Margaret Whitlam who had one too. By Peter Thompson for *Talking Heads*, by Stewart Littlemore for a one-off *Media Watch*, by Clive James, Andrew Denton and even insufferably pompous William F. Buckley Jr. But you knew you were safe with Michael. He might never have taken risks – but you weren't at risk either.

Vale Parky.

Julian

I was introduced to Julian Assange years before Wikileaks, when he was a child-prodigy computer hacker blowing electric raspberries at the authorities. To borrow from the Pythons he wasn't the Messiah but a very naughty boy'. Eccentric, yes. He may be 'on the spectrum'. But I liked him immediately – and a lot.

So when a few years later Julian told me of his idea – and ideals – for Wikileaks, a freelance 'freedom of information' service on a global scale – and asked me to be the Australian representative on the grand sounding 'International Advisory Board' I was honoured to accept. Though let the record show the Board has never met, either in reality or virtually. Neither has Julian ever sought my advice.

The only consequence for my association with Wikileaks was the Trump's government's refusal to grant a visa to the US. (I'm used to visa problems, having been denied permission to return to both China or India for the sin of being a journalist). But the consequences for Julian? Never-ending incarceration and torture.

I consider Julian a dear friend – and have become friends with his mother, father and wife. Not a day passes when I do not think of him and his sufferings and fear for his future life – and death – in an American SuperMax prison. If he lives that long given evidence that the CIA has or had plans to kill him.

This Australian citizen has been effectively abandoned by his own government. Since PM Gillard notoriously echoed the US line on Assange (just as Australian PMs echo the US on most things as evidenced most recently by AUKUS) every government has failed him. The conservatives don't give a damn – and Albanese asked us to be patient. This was no time for megaphone diplomacy. Trust us to obtain his freedom via back channels. From time to time an announcement seemed imminent – you might recall journo John Lyons's confident assertion that the gates of Belmarsh were about to swing open. They didn't'. Now Ambassador Kennedy hints that a 'plea bargain' may be on the table – but few would trust a government that wants him dead, one way or the other. Since Barack Obama pardoned Chelsea Manning who provided Wikileaks with the evidence of US war crimes, the White House has been obdurate. Our bestie Biden is no better than Trump.

Countless Australians have banded together to fight for Julian – John Pilger, Yanis Varoufakis, ex Foreign Minister Bob Carr and human rights lawyer Geoffrey Robertson. I backed a petition signed by almost a million. We've written books, organised rallies and, made documentaries in the campaign to save Julian's sanity and his life – efforts in which were joined by his heroic predecessor, the great whistle-blower Daniel Ellsberg. Recently, numbers of national leaders have called upon the US for his release. No response.

The last time I saw Julian was in the Ecuadorian Embassy in London where I feared for his physical and mental health. Back then he listened to my radio program every night – said it kept him 'in touch with Australia'. We sometimes talked on air. None of that in Belmarsh, where he's effectively been in solitary confinement for years. Extradition is imminent – with perhaps a reprieve from a Starmer government?

Assange's 'crime' deserves the Nobel Peace Prize. He told the world about US war crimes. Now Julian's personal Doomsday Clock is seconds from midnight.

Horrorscope

At the last census astronomers guesstimated that there are 200 billion trillion stars. Astrologers ignore the maths and focus on about a dozen, assigning to them magical powers to influence our daily lives. Voila your horoscope! Think of its predictions as a weather forecast for your personal future.

Experience suggests that these forecasts are not quite as reliable as those provided by the Bureau of Meteorology. Which is why I've tended to ignore the horoscopic effects of astrologers published in newspapers and magazines. Nor am I in the habit of messing with the entrails of owls. Truth is I've never wanted to peak into my future. On past experience it wouldn't be too fancy. Better not to know.

Had I read my horoscope a decade or so ago it would have been a horrorscope.

Among the nasty surprises that lay ahead? 1. Deafness, 2. Macular degeneration – needing surgery and monthly eye jabs, 3. Multiple starring appearances in operating theatres for removals and replacements – including artificial hips, 4. Heart troubles requiring the implanting of pacemakers, 5. The Near-Death Experience of cancer, 6. A few painful encounters with gravity and, 7. Like so many of us, the vicissitudes of Covid. I could add numbers 8-11 but you get the picture.

This brings me to another horrorscope – involving life and death on the farm. Plagues galore. A Biblical infestation of locusts was the least of our troubles. Far more destructive were mice and rats – the latter munching the wiring in cars and 4WDs. A hurricane ripped off roofs, crushed vehicles and ringbarked a thousand trees. Varroa mites attacked our beloved hives. We lost six much-loved dogs to snake bite. And a continuing onslaught of feral pigs makes rabbits seem welcome.

Disasters of a larger scale – the long-predicted impacts of climate change. Vast droughts, those bushfires in slow motion – that killed everything from cattle to crops – from leaves of grass to giant, century-old trees that once sheltered the Elmswood homestead. Heart-breaking. And as I write these words of woe and worry another drought has commenced. Bushfires? We've had our share – and are now scanning the horizon for signs of smoke.

Drought punctuated by floods of unprecedented frequency and scale, wreaking havoc as they wreck the riverbanks and bury the bridge in detritus. If it's not one damn thing it's another. Or both.

And climate change is happening everywhere to everyone. Wars raging across the planet, the threat of nuclear weapons has the Doomsday Clock just seconds to midnight. But the climate catastrophe, this self-inflicted war on our planet, makes a Third World War look trivial.

And god knows what other plagues and epidemics will emerge. Certainly there'll be wars over water as there were once wars over oil. Not merely waves but tsunamis of refugees will soon dwarf any in human history. You don't need an astrologer to tell you that. Ask your insurance actuaries or statisticians. The writing's on the wall or in the computer modelling.

Christian fundamentalists believe we're living in the End Times. The Final Judgement looms with Pentacostalists rapturous about the rapture. And this old atheist? He feels almost fortunate to be heading for the exit.

Yep, the Final Judgement on our human stewardship of this dilapidated planet looms. And it looks like we'll all be found guilty – and given the death sentence.

Hence my reluctance to read the horrors of the horoscope. Have a nice day.

Australia Rhymes with Failure

Australia rhymes with failure. Some jokingly suggested that's why we've such a woeful national anthem. But the Australia/failure connection runs far and wide and deep.

For example: long before controversially declaring January 26th as Australia Day, our real national day was, yes, Anzac Day in which we pay tribute to a monumental military defeat. The One Day of the Year celebrates and mythologises… failure.

If Advance Australia is a failure as our official anthem our beloved unofficial anthem, Waltzing Matilda, is a sad and sorry song of failure. A dirge about a swagman who hurls himself into a billabong to drown – nothing 'jolly' about him. This was no historic gesture of political principle. The swaggie commits suicide over a stolen jumbuck. Rather than face the wrath of the squatter mounted on his thoroughbred – and the accompanying troopers – he condemns himself to death. Surely to die over the possession of a shabby sheep is a failure.

Talking of the death penalty takes us from the ghostly presence of the swaggie to another anti-heroic failure, our beloved bushranger Ned Kelly, who comes off second best with the cops and is doomed to die on a scaffold. His last words, we're told, were an embittered 'Such is life!'. Failure, failure, failure.

Add to the roll call of failures the seemingly endless numbers of brave and bold explorers who perished in the deserts. Perhaps most infamously those famous failures Burke and Wills.

The life of Phar Lap, Australia's most famous horse, ends in his premature death. Ditto, another champion, Les Darcy.

Fifty years ago I wrote a column about how the principal characters in our New Wave feature films invariably end in failure. Jack Thompson made it a sub-genre – he wanted to be the gun shearer in *Sunday Too Far Away* – and fails. He tried to save Breaker Morant from the firing squad – and failed. In *Peterson* Jack's character wants to be successful at university – and finishes up repairing TV sets. And what became of the girls in *Picnic*? They fail to return.

In US films the heroes almost invariably win the battle, get the girl and ride off into the sunset. In Australia, for the first decade of our reborn film industry, they're flops.

We've failed to have an independent voice in foreign affairs – joining the US in its succession of failed wars. Vietnam, Iraq, Afghanistan. We were once a significant manufacturer – producing, for example, the majority of our own cars. Choosing between Ford or Holden was almost religious – like being Catholic vs Protestant. Finally our auto industry failed.

In recent memory Australia failed to become a Republic. We failed at Reconciliation. We failed to treat refugees with humanity. We failed to defeat our own denialists in effectively tackling climate change. The impact of this failure is evidenced in flood and fire and our re-entry into devastating drought.

But for many our greatest national failure has been our treatment of the First Australians. Two centuries of abuse, massacres, rapes, poisoning, enslavement, displacement, incarceration, introduced disease – and stolen children. Closing the gap? Look at the stats on indigenous health and life expectancy.

And finally, in a dark victory for bigotry and wilful ignorance, we failed to pass the Voice.

Even before the treasonable Trump I was describing the US, in broadcast and columns, as a Failed State. Let's hope that Australia can avoid that designation.

Dig Deep

I have never met David Berenson. We have never spoken. I haven't even seen a photograph of him. And yet we are friends and I know him very well because of his remarkable writings.

David has been sending me fragments of his prose for some years now. Sometimes one or two emails a day, sometimes weeks apart. And when David's back in hospital, extended and worrying silences.

David, fighting his personal Goliath of disability, writes with such raw passion that it overwhelms grammar and spelling and his punctuation is wildly erratic. To which I respond with 'tidy-up' suggestions. But in my efforts at editing I have never touched his content, his 'tales from the depths'.

I met David via my daughter – Dr Rebecca Adams – a psychiatrist practising in Melbourne. He is Rebecca's friend, not her patient. She marvelled at his writings, seeing them not merely as therapeutic for David but potentially for anyone fortunate enough to read them. I agree. We are privileged to share David's utter honesty in his thoughts and observations. On life, on death, on disability, on friendship, on literally hundreds upon hundreds of subjects.

While David truly speaks to 'the human condition' his writings are not bleak. Despite his profound problems he is undaunted, forever hopeful and frequently very funny. His book is called *Dig Deep, Tales from the Depths*. It is published by Franklin Street Press and I wholeheartedly commend it to you. And I also commend the efforts of Gary Sturgess. Gary has painstakingly decoded David's writings when his emotions overwhelm his clarity.

As I turn the pages of *Dig Deep* I find paragraphs on every imaginable and unimaginable topic. For example... Pizza, Rabbi Bugel, Uncle Croissant, Lost and Found, the Piano, Heart Attack, Gianthood, Acland Street, A Birthday, School, The Teacher, The Drug Addict, Anzac Day, The Future of Life, Uni, The Train Trip, Bang – The Accident, Brave New World, Near Life Experience, The Doctor Won't See You Now, The Drink of Life, Body Image, The Longest Journey, The Cone of Silence, Isolation, All Is Not Lost, Thanks NDIS, Being Me, First Nation, The Dreamtime, Bookshops, My Brain, Life's Perpetual Challenge, Am I Valuable!, Patience, Friendship, My Mates, Shared Journeys, the Undead, Covid Coffee, Cake Shops, The Doughnut, Hebrew. Dozens and dozens of mini-titles that read like blank verse. They're a pleasure in themselves as each page arrives – and many of them are not much longer than a single paragraph – I read them not with pity but with pleasure. I've always found it an honour that David shares them with me, as well as with Rebecca and Gary Sturgess.

But let David speak for himself.

'I have developed a two-pronged approach to writing. Through the storytelling, I produce what might be called faction, a combination of fact and fiction. To produce faction I need to muse aloud and let my mind wander where it will. While doing this I feel my ego straining at the leash. It is very difficult to restrain myself and maintain humility.

'When writing I think of myself as an open window into my mind. Through the window you may see a mirrored wall, reflecting compartments of my mind with their overlay of images and realities... My aim is to build a picture that enables people to get inside my mind and see how it functions... I hope that readers find it contributes value to the way in which they confront the complexities of their own lives. My book is rather simple – the perspectives of an educated man modified by his life experiences in all its dimensions... What I offer is a composite of many things…

Over the years many people have said to me, 'David, you should write your story.' My instinctive response has been, 'Why bother?' I am nothing special.

But, of course, David is special.

When David writes 'From the Depths' it is not from the depths of despair but from the depths of his experience. His disabilities came suddenly – in a terrible accident – whereas other disabilities come in increments. That has certainly been my experience as one by one my own senses dim. First my hearing, now my sight. And thanks to modern medicine my heart keeps ticking over with an implanted pacemaker – and I try to navigate the world with artificial hips. So, increasingly, I empathise with David Berenson and admire his hard-won wisdom. I invite you to enter his world. For all his problems, for all his 'issues', it can be a magical place.

2024

Times

It is a sign of the times, of your own personal times, that you'd like everyone to wear name tags. Even friends and family. Particularly family. And perhaps pets.

Unlike newfangled smart phones we octogenarians lose our facial recognition skills. Who owns this visage? Who are you? Do I know you? If so, why?

And that's not the only problem we have with names. Our 'contacts' contain hundreds of names we don't remember. Why are they there? Take Peter. I've a lot of Peters in my life but the phone proffers scores more. No hint of their significance. And that's before the even worse problem of the 'contacts' I can't contact. Because they're dead. And soon they'll be the silent majority.

Every day I feel a pulse and check the obits to see if I'm still alive. As of now, yes. Or more accurately more or less. But I find myself beginning more and more radio programs or tweets with 'vale'. On into the vale of death.

In the last few weeks I've lost two John friends – Pilger and Embling. But the uncountable in my 'contacts' has a dozen other ex-Johns. Which leads to a multi-horned dilemma. Should I delete them as life has? Seems rude really, a final metaphor nail on their coffins.

Until Wikipedia put it out of busines I subscribed to *Who's Who In Australia*. Every year a thick, thumping and expensive volume would arrive with faux leather binding and I found it useful – and more reliable than Wikipedia with its faux facts. For example, I hardly recognize myself. It's so out of date and abbreviated you'd get more info on a Fantail wrapper.

But now *Who's Who* is no more. The voluminous volumes sit as silent and unopened as that other victim of Wikipedia, the *Encylopaedia Britannica*. I only mention *Who's Who* for one reason: the way it is deals with death.

They took their title seriously. It was present tense. Who's Who – not Who Was. Once you were dead your entry was buried, cremated, forgotten. No matter how august you were in life, no matter how many honours, gongs or medals you'd accrued, your death meant your deletion. You were exiled, expelled, expired, executed and shown the exit. The ex fell. You were as ex as John Cleese's parrot.

Like our overcrowded cemeteries there's no more room for more in my iPhone. So do I follow *Who's Who*'s rigorous example with my overcrowded contacts? Use a sort of contact lens not to shed but shed the dead? Should I, dear reader, press the delete button? Or let them linger on in a sort of half-life? Or try to ring them still? In the hope there's Wi-Fi in the thereafter? Could I, at least, leave a message?

Perhaps there's a telephonic limbo, a 5G purgatory? And would I know given our lousy NBN connection?

A confession. There are many alive-and-kicking contacts, including a plethora of politicians, I'd be delighted to delete. Particularly if it proved fatal. And many more I'd like to block as you can with Elon's Twitter – or X... another form of eX?

Of course my computer allows me to Restore – to backtrack on deletions. And there's a lot of contacts I'd love to retore, resurrect.

Your views would be appreciated. Preferred protocols? Post-mortem manners? But be prompt in making contact. My time – and perhaps yours – is running out.

The Interview

Although we've been close for 84 years I'd never actually talked to him/her/it. But finally Australia granted me an exclusive interview.

I've observed in the past that Australia looks like a vast pair of buttocks hovering over the cold toilet seat of the Antarctic with Perth and Sydney at the hips and Adelaide serving as sphincter. This is not an image that flatters Tasmania and for that I fully apologise.

Anyway Australia and I sat down together. We started with the usual small talk. How was the southern continent feeling? 'A bit off' came the reply. 'Hot flushes. No, nothing menopausal. It's because of climate change. Running a high temperature'.

Australia muttered that they should stop digging him/her/it up for fossil fuels and go for renewables 'Much less discomfort. How would you feel having your flesh constantly gouged by coal miners? It's bad enough being ravished by Gina and Twiggy'.

Two more shudders.

Time to placate. It is polite for a guest to bring a gift and I'd brought the latest demographics. Human population? Nudging 26,000,00 (a figure that caused Australia to give a painful moan – as did the thought of 25,000,000 head of cattle). Then to traditional occupants – with twice as many kangaroos as us. The population of Reds, Eastern Greys and others (here I asked Australia to forgive an unforgivable pun) was leaping. Sadly kangas are topped by 70,000,000 sheep. 'Too many mouths to feed' moaned Australia. I didn't have the heart to mention a million feral camels.

Though it's impolite to ask someone their age I couldn't resist. A huffy response. '200 years according to that silly day named after me.

Fifty thousand or more according to the Aboriginal people.' 'Now, how old are YOU?'

This led to a wandering conversation on the wanderings of Gondwanaland and other supercontinents. 'It seems only a few billion years since I was connected to Antarctica, India, Africa and South America', Australia said in a voice soggy with sentiment – less so about the painful grinding of tectonic plates. ('I'm thinking about hip replacements'). We're talking of the time when fossil fuels were being mass produced but I was reluctant to return to that unhappy topic. 'How I miss Pangea', Australia sighed.

Australia is home to the oldest rocks of terrestrial origin. Found in WA (but don't tell Ms Rinehart lest she dig them up and export them) they're 4,400 billion years old. This is the same age as our continental crust, again the world's oldest.

Now Australia's mood had changed – a vast rumbling wasn't volcanic but a purr of pride and pleasure.

'You realise', said Australia, 'If I've got the maths right that's about the same age as the Moon!'.

(In contrast that heart-breaking Uluru, though far bigger than the W.A brinnies, is a recent arrival, fully 4 billion years younger).

We spent the next hour reminiscing about his/her/its old days. 'I've seen it all young Adams. Climate changes galore, the whole place covered in ice, mega-fires, megafauna, mass extinctions. The lot'.

So much for the past. What of the future for Australia? 'I don't think your mob has one. The stats for humans, sheep, cattle, kangaroos and feral camels will be, very sadly, very different – and very soon.'

At which point Australia sighed, stood up and walked slowly, stiffly away.

Who Killed Julius Ceasar?

As you know, beloved reader, true crime podcasting is all the go. For example, it has been adopted by everyone with the surname Thomas. This masthead's Hedley Thomas is a master of the craft – and my erstwhile producer at LNL, Helen Thomas, is offering a fresh look at a very cold case, the notorious Easey Street murders in Melbourne. And a fellow called Dylan Thomas is tackling the mid-summer-style murders in his Welsh fishing village.

I must confess a certain pride in my own True Crime output. My 'Who Really Killed…?' series has attracted millions of downloads. Who Really Killed Franz Joseph? Who Really Killed Mahatma Gandhi? Who Really Killed Martin Luther King? Who Really Killed John Lennon? Who Really Killed Trotsky in Mexico? Czar Nicholas in St Petersburg? Malcolm X? Bobby Kennedy? And, of course, Who Really Killed JFK? Having disposed of scores of silly conspiracy theories I confirm that the Warren Commission was a whitewash and that the real culprit, the person who organised 'the hit' was Lyndon Baines Johnson. Impatient at being a mere VP he plotted to be POTUS. And given that he and brother Bobby detested each other I suspect LBJ was implicated in that subsequent assassination of RFK.

Then there's my more subtle series of the 'almost assassinations'. Of course every second president has almost been assassinated – most notably Ronald Reagan. And even George W Bush. But to be honest they don't attract as wide an audience as the four whammies.

Which brings us to my latest and perhaps greatest. Who Really Killed Julius Caesar? But first, some context.

The ABC psephologist is also our resident astrologist. This latter gift helps explain his uncanny ability to predict election outcomes. Moreover outgoing Chair Ita Buttrose never made a major decision without having Anthony run the numbers.

It was Anthony who brought to my attention that Julius Caesar and I share the same birth date, 12 July. Mine was 1939, his a few thousand years earlier. Anthony showed me this astrological link on the Ides of March which, of course, passed recently and was the date of what Spike Milligan called his 'dreaded deadings'. There were oodles of eye-witnesses but, of course, eye-witness testimony is notoriously unreliable. Everyone says the brute who committed the brutal act was Brutus. And that Caesar's last words were 'And you Brutus? Then I shall come a cropper.' Or words to that effect in Latin.

But I recently came in possession of Caesar's rent and blooded garment. Yes, its survival is every bit as miraculous as that of the Shroud of Turin and a DNA lab in Brisbane was able to extract the vital information that points neither to Brutus nor that thin and hungry deep-thinking Cassius. Shockingly, amazingly, the evidence suggests that the murder was carried out by his alleged bestie, Marc Antony, so vividly portrayed by Marlon Brando in the bio pic.

Under Freedom of Information I also obtained fingerprint data from the FBI (the forum's bureau of investigation) with a 9-point match to Antony. He had the chutzpah to stand over the bleeding corpse and proclaim that he was 'here not to praise Caesar but to bury him' – when in fact he arranged his mentor's murder. The ploy was a simple one and excuses the observations of the many witnesses. Antony described himself as Brutus.

I'll concede that my discoveries demand the rewriting of history as well as one of Shakespeare's better plays. But so be it. Let the cards fall where they may.

I see myself performing an important role – like the recent series *Nemesis*, which provided a sorry tale of political if not physical assassinations. Effecting this nation's Liberal Caesars.

In my next True Crime podcast I shall reveal the true identity of Jack the Ripper and, just as Epstein led us to Prince Andrew, the Jack the Ripper evidence leads us to Prince Albert. This will come as a considerable embarrassment to Buckingham Palace.

Roo

Consider, fellow patriots, the kangaroo. They're the large animals on the left on our coat of arms, opposite the giant chooks. Coming in various shapes and sizes they're called macropods, meaning 'big foot'. Not to be confused with Bigfoot the elusive and perhaps mythical bipedal critter that hides in the forests of North America.

At last count there were about 50,000,000 macropods in Australia, and there are times when a majority of them seem to live on Elmswood Farm in the Upper Hunter. Droughts take a terrible toll on their numbers – lack of water, lack of feed – but during boomtimes for boomers it's a sad necessity to cull them – 'cull' being a weasel word for kill.

On one such occasion I found a very young orphaned joey chitterring and shivering besides its dead mum and, managing to catch it, took it back to the homestead. After advice from the local vet I began to mother it – giving it two-hourly bottle-feeds.

I made a pouch out of an old black skivvie where it spent the nights. It would summersault into the skivvie dangling from the door handle of the laundry. But in waking hours it followed me everywhere. And I mean everywhere.

It would, for example, hop into the shower with me. And it'd sit beside me for our weekly 300 km commute between Sydney and the bush. Looking happily out the window.

At the time I was Chair of the Australian Film Commission and a trainee shock-jock at 2UE with cash-for-commenting colleagues John Laws, Alan Jones and Stan Zemanek. My joey became a familiar sight, hopping around the studios.

In my AFC role I had to welcome a cultural delegation of Chinese film makers who delighted in having group and solo photos taken with my pet. As did a rising-star pollie called Paul Keating. Paul was cradling the joey in his arms when she piddled all over him, causing some damage to his Zegna suit.

Back in the bush she continued to grow and soon was hearing the call of the wild. She'd hop off into the hills for the day, returning to home and the black skivvie around sunset. Soon her absences grew longer until she left permanently, rejoining her mob of Eastern Greys, one of the four species of roo and wallaby cohabiting the 10,000 acres. Never, as far as we know, to be seen again.

One night, returning at the usual 3 am, I found a kangaroo in the garage. My heart leapt – but it wasn't her. It was a badly injured old feller who'd clearly lost his last battle for supremacy. Counterintuitively braving electric fences and our dogs to seek refuge in human company. No chance he'd ever been a pet – farmers don't attempt to tame male joeys as they can grow pretty dangerous.

(We know this from personal experience having been attacked by a six-footer – and having a beloved dog killed by another.)

At first the refugee wouldn't let anyone near him, but over the weeks of giving him food and water, he'd permit me to approach. Then touch. Finally it died while I cradled its head.

What became of my baby? The life expectancy of a roo in the wild is just 8 years. Whereas a roo living with humans can keep hopping around for 25. So leaving home was not merely ungrateful but a bad career choice.

Vale m'dear. Come to think of it we never gave you a name.

Exit Stage Left

At 11pm on Thursday night David Anderson, CEO of the 'taxpayer-funded ABC' (as Gerard Henderson invariably describes it) unceremoniously dumped me on the footpath at 700 Harris Street Ultimo for council collection. No, that's not accurate. Some ceremony was attached – taking the form of a final interview. Not conducted by me but by staff-elected board member Laura Tingle with Adams, the ancient broadcaster as her interviewee, guest or victim.

On most Monday nights for decades I've discussed our oft disgusting politics with Laura. This was my final 'mingle with Tingle'.

On other nights I've talked with Bruce Shapiro on the rancid politics of the Failed State – calling these encounters on the US 'Shapirouette's, or 'being blunt with Dunt', the percussive Ian Dunt on the UK. No more.

As an advocate of voluntary euthanasia, I've gone willingly. I will now suffer from PBD (post broadcasting disorder) and RD (relevance deprivation) although I may dull the pain of the latter by suing someone, anyone for defamation.

Thus endeth a career of over 50 years in wireless, 33 in public broadcasting, after previous and traumatic experience in shock-jockery with the likes of cash-for-commentators Laws and Jones. As Ned said on the gibbet 'Such is life'.

Since taking over from previous presenter Virginia Bell – who went on to become a High Court judge – LNL has gone to air around 14,000 times, forcing me into close proximity to a pantheon of PMs, presidents and potentates plus a plethora if not a plague of professors. Plus Nobel laureates by the score. *Guinness Book of Records* stuff. Pick a name, any name. Arthur? I give you Arthur Miller, Arthur C. Clarke and Arthur Schlesinger Jr. The good, the bad and the ugly have included everyone from Kissinger to Gorbachev. To list the notables and the notorieties living and dead would require every page in the *Oz*, not just the Magazine. It'd be easier to list those I haven't interviewed. Only God and John Howard.

Various forms of life-after-professional-death have been arranged by compassionate colleagues in the form of archival websites available for downloads. And I shall linger on in X via what used to be tweets. Uninhibited by ABC rules-and-regs and self-censorship. As I am here, on this page.

Thanks to all my countless thousands of guests, regulars and randoms. Thanks to my valiant EPs and brilliant producers who did the decades of heavy lifting that made our 'little wireless program' possible. Thanks to my beloved listeners, the Gladdies who've put up with me since the late 19th century. And good luck to my lucky successor David Marr who inherits the best job in Australian media. The only program that allows you to interview anyone anywhere about anything.

PS. Why call my listeners Gladys? Two reasons. Firstly I see radio as the most intimate medium – essentially one-on-one. The other one being Gladys. Secondly, coming to RN from 2UE meant I was free from the tyranny and endless dread of ratings.

Management deplored my Gladys idea and ordered me to cease and desist. I disobeyed and it caught on. I've a fond memory of a bloke as big as the proverbial brick dunny blocking a footpath and gruffly growling 'G'day Phil. I'm Gladys'. And a full house at the Perth Town Hall where thousands wearing badges proclaiming 'I'm Gladys'. Shades of 'I'm Spartacus'.

Over and out.

Friends

Once upon a time in Australian politics friendships transcended parties. I remember when a conservative like Menzies could be on very cordial terms with a lefty like Jim Cairns – and when Sir Robert was grief-stricken by the death of Chifley.

When the like of lefties like me could like truly liberal Liberals like Alan Missen, Margaret Guilfoyle, Fred Chaney – and an eccentric like Jim Killen. On some issues we could make common cause.

I also remember a time when there were love affairs across party lines, most delightfully a Montagu-Capulet romance in the Senate. Equally I recall detesting some on my side of politics – the mendacious Mark Latham and the Senator McClelland who wasn't Jim.

I was particularly friendly with the liberal Lib Philip Ruddock – admiring the way he'd cross the floor on a point of principle – and for setting up a parliamentary branch of that admirable organisation Amnesty International – proudly wore its badge on his lapel. Its ideals symbolised by a burning candle shining through barbed wire. Imagine my disappointment when, as a member of the Howard government, he started putting refugees behind barbed wire. And blowing out the candle.

When Amnesty demanded he remove the badge Phil refused. Perhaps he's still wearing it today.

I visited Phil in his office. 'How can you be party to this?' A long silence. Finally he said, 'I've waited twenty years to be a minister.' Let that, dear reader, sink in.

A voice from an era when JWH purged the party of so-called 'wets'. It was his way or the highway. Now the Libs are dryer than the Millennial Drought.

In earlier days I'd worked with 'wets' – with that liberal Liberal Don Chipp fighting the good fight against Australia's notorious censorship of literature and cinema. When Don couldn't rally the Libs behind he formed the Australian Democrats – and I happily campaigned for him. For a while the Dems kept their promise 'to keep the bastards honest'. A precursor to the Teals?

The Howard purges inflicted mortal damage on his party – still does decades later. I could list a score of notables these in Liberal history who would never get preselection in Dutton's day. The party moved to far to the right that Menzies must be rolling in his proverbial grave. The Liberal Party? The name is a much false advertising as my coinage 'the Spirit of Australia' is in Qantas campaigns. The Libs are, all too often, echoes of Trump's Republicans.

And the ALP? On Albo's front bench we see many who'd have Gough too spinning in his grave. Whitlam's principles have been as dismissed like his government was by Kerr. Can you imagine EGW signing up for AUKUS? It getting through caucus? Or such vacillations on Gaza?

Everybody's favourite Marxists – Harpo, Chico and most notably Groucho – come to mind. What was his great one-liner? (Well, actually a two-liner), 'You don't like my principles? I have others'.

(There's little left of the Left. Having resigned from the Labor Party over the coup against Kevin I've never seen sufficient reason to re-join.)

All the above feeds into the general cynicism the young feel for politics. And that's before you factor in the lunatic fringe of One Nation, the Nats and their ilk. As seen in the destruction of The Voice and the criminal inaction on the Climate Crisis.

Honestly, I'm rolling in my grave.

End Times

In the early 80s, as the newly designated chair of Barry Jones' Commission for the Future, an organisation dedicated to bringing together scientists, pollies and the public – in the hope of better long-term policies – I sought advice from some of our greatest scientific minds.

At a formal dinner in Canberra I asked this simple, ominous question. 'How will the world end? With a bang or a whimper?'

The Cold War was very cold – the Doomsday Clock near midnight – and the doomed War on Drugs was underway. DNA's discoveries, including GMOs, were in their infancy. Ditto the Internet. The mass media had yet to be disrupted, social media to turn the iPhone into a physical (and mental) appendage. The human's 'opposed thumb' into the connection. Elon Musk was a baby.

One by one the scientists counted down the existential threats – unsurprisingly beginning with nuclear war. Next came the fear we'd render ourselves redundant. This prospect was vividly imagined prior to the invention of GM and AI. Either or both unnamed technologies could reduce humans to, at best, the status of pets. Or creatures of curiosity to be kept in zoos.

Note: no one mentioned pandemics. But the final threat, then unknown to some at table, was the inexorable rise in carbon dioxide. After listening to the story of the time-bomb tick of rising carbon dioxide in their colleague's laboratory – and in labs around the world – a consensus emerged. The evening ended with total agreement.

The Commission for the Future must first and foremost warn Australia of the Greenhouse Effect. So we organised national and international conferences on what would become Global Warming and, later, Climate Change. Way back in the 1980s we linked Town Hall meetings around Australia via primitive satellite links, beaming in global and local experts.

Off to a flying start? Thanks to a fatal combination of fossil fuel industry chicanery, wilful ignorance, determined and continuing denialism and delaying tactics by gutless governments… to little effect.

Fast forward from the 1980s to 2024. Nuclear War still threatens – again the Doomsday Clock is second from midnight, its ticking now hastened by including the Climate Crisis (the latest term) in its dread calculations. The US-declared War on Drugs continues to wreak havoc on populations and entire nations. GM crops increase and the bees are dying. And AI is on the march, marching us to the abyss.

The Climate Crisis – or Climate Emergency – worsens by the hour. Bigger storms, deeper droughts, fiercer fires, coral bleaching, mass extinctions. Already Pacific nations are imperilled by rising sea levels. Ditto Bangladesh. This will be the century of countless millions of environmental refugees.

Apart from the self-inflicted wounds from climate change denialism the wounds of the War on Drugs, arguably our greatest public policy fiasco, continues to criminalise the pandemics of addiction, causing unprecedented corruption, clogging policing and court systems and overcrowding prisons. (Sorry to spend so much space on this issue. The US clearly repressed the memories of Prohibition).

Genuine pandemics, old and new, are in the wind – like chemical pollutant their air we breathe, and our water, oceans and food. Wars rage in Ukraine and Gaza. And joy of joys, Donald Trump may win (sic) a second term in the Failed Sate of the US.

Seems the only thing we learn from history is how to repeat it. Well, it was a nice planet while we had it.

Crash

Elmswood, our home for the past 40 years, stands on a hill overlooking the merging of two rivers, the Isis and the Pages, that blend downstream with the Hunter.

This is Wonnarua Country. Before white settlement 100 ancient carved trees once stood at our river's edge.

Built around 130 years ago, our classic Victorian homestead is a two-story brick design, not counting attics and cellars, surrounded by verandas with traditional wrought-iron embellishments.

Keeping the homestead close company for much of its history – as it turns out too close – is or were three enormous Celtis trees – soaring above to give shade. They were planted by the original owners, who, we suspect, thought they were elms. Growing ever larger, surviving epic droughts and hurricanes, until, one recent night, with reverberations that must have registered on the Richter Scale, half the largest and the closest came crashing down. Had it fallen at a slightly different angle, it would have been the world's largest indoor plant.

This week, Will, Benson and Florian, the young 'Climbcare' team, in high-vis and helmets, have been dangling from ropes, skilfully chain-sawing mighty and minor branches to feed into a thundering wood-chipping machine. We now have mountains of chips that will be used to mulch other old and ailing trees. But Elmswood looks very sad, and we are in deep mourning.

Droughts have killed hundreds of lesser trees, while a recent hurricane, roaring like a vast bulldozer, ring-barked hundreds more. Lightning strikes have also taken their toll. Ditto bushfires. With their high mortality rate the planting of new trees can't keep up. And now there's the Climate Crisis, intensifying drought and bushfires.

Yes, we're tree-huggers who love trees deeply, and I write about them often. I've described my friendship with a gnarled peppercorn on the tiny farm where I grew up – and have written columns demanding that trees get the vote – imagining a Larboreal Party taking over from Labor. And I've made woeful jokes about branch stacking and handing out how-to-vote leaflets, including gumleaflets. I vaguely recall an awful pun about 'Donald Trunk for President', for which I apologise

Meanwhile, we slaughter Australian trees in their millions, not only via increasingly epic bushfires but by what's euphemistically known as 'land clearing.' That's a proud tradition of Australian colonialism, immortalised in the maxim 'If it's moving, shoot it, if it's standing still, cut it down.'

It's as bad across the region where the skies darken as tropical forests are torched to make space for palm oil plantations. And grimmest of all in the Amazon Basin, accurately described as 'the lungs of the world'. We depend on trees for the very air we breathe. Simple maths – no trees, no oxygen.

Though no greenie, PM Bob Hawke promised to plant a billion trees. That's nowhere near enough. It doesn't replace the losses in the last bushfires. We need at least that number to restore the habitats of endangered species – think koalas.

Yet we continue deforestation. Look to the horror story going on in Tasmania – at the logging of ancient forests, much of it for the effing woodchip industry.

So give trees the vote – they'd certainly get mine. Eucalypts for the Senate! Wattles for the Reps! Angophoras in state parliaments!

'I think that I shall never see a poem as lovely as a tree,' wrote American Joyce Kilmer in 1913. There's not a lot of poetry in a stump.

Tony

On balance Tony is my favourite politician. No, neither Tony Abbott nor Tony Blair. All hail the remarkable Tony Benn, the Viscount who gave up his title to become a working-class hero in UK politics, the conscience of his party and the bane of his near namesake in Number 10.

You've met Benn before on this page – and will find examples of his oratorial brilliance on YouTube. And each year I return to examine and update the political theory Tony vouchsafed me twenty years ago. He holds that all politicians, irrespective of place, time in history or form of politics, come in one of three categories. 1. Straight, 2. Fixer, 3. Maddie.

Applied to British PMs the Straights might include John Major, Harold Wilson, Ted Heath and perhaps the new bloke Keir Starmer. The Fixers? And note that they don't always succeed at fixing (more oft than not they break things) include Blair, Cameron and a few of David's short-lived successors like Rishi.

The Maddies? Those who for good and ill change things? Churchill, Thatcher, Johnson.

In the rapidly accelerating roll-call of Australian PMs? Menzies was the great Fixer. Curtin and Chifley? Straights. And I'd include Whitlam here – because of his quite formal attitudes to the political rules and regulations. Gough was a Straight who did great things.

Maddies? That maddening opportunist Malcolm Frazer. Tony Abbott – they don't call him 'the Mad Monk' for nothing. And the Maddies' Maddie? Scott Morrison, the religious nutter with multiple ministry disorder. Albanese? Straight – not a great Fixer. Howard – the PM who wanted to look Straight, broke things as a Fixer and, in company with Maddie George W Bush, did some of the maddest things in modern history.

Rudd? Straight. Gillard and Turnbull? Faulty fixers. Keating? Labor's greatest Maddie – who when thus described in this column rang me from the Lodge purring with pleasure.

USA? FDR – his nation's greatest Fixer. Truman? Straight. Ditto Eisenhower. Nixon? The Fixer who went utterly mad. Reagan? Looked Straight but an ultra-Maddie. George H Bush – a Straight. Gerald Ford? An inept Straight. Bill Clinton? A sleazy Fixer. The inspirational Obama – a Fixer who sadly disappointed.

Donald Trump is in a category all his own. He is the fake-gold standard in Maddies. That monstrous mendacious miscreant. Versus the monochromatic Biden, a broken Fixer.

Soviet Union and Russia? Stalin was as much a Maddie as Hitler. Gorbachev, the Fixer who broke the USSR into pieces – for which most Russians never forgave him. Particularly Vladimir Putin – determined to Make Russia Great Again. The latest Moscow Maddie.

Neville Wran takes the cake for Australian fixing. He's not called Nifty for nothing. Which serves to remind us that all three of Benn's categories have their merits. It's good to have incorruptible Straights, and there is much needing a Fixer's repairs. And from time to time we can benefit from the Maddie.

So where to put Benn on his spectrum? He believed politics should be straighter, the better to fix things. So he was probably mad.

Among my favourite Benn quotes: 'Hope is the fuel of progress and fear is the prison in which you put yourself.' 'It's the same each time with progress. First they ignore you, then they say you're mad, then there's a pause, and then you can't find anyone to disagree with you.'

This column is dedicated to his memory. Tony Benn, 1925 to 2014.

Happy Birthday?

T*he Guinness Book of Records* reckons Happy Birthday to You is the world's most recognised song. It is probably the most often sung as well, and in my view also qualifies as the worst song ever written.

When reluctantly turning 85, I was subjected to several well-intentioned solo and choral performances and marvelled at the dirge's popularity. Consider the lyrics – hardly of Gershwin, Hammerstein, Porter, Berlin or Coward quality. The same words are thrice repeated with "happy birthday to (fill this space)" the only subtle variant. Talk about easy to memorise.

Only the comparably repetitive God Save the King comes close – making it the second worst song in the history of the known universe. But more on the Brit's bathetic National Anthem later.

Who on earth would want to take credit for Happy Birthday's lamentable libretto? Believe it or not, Mildred and Patty Hill claim they wrote it in 1893. And believe it or not, the damnable dirge is still embroiled in copyright lawsuits – with demands for royalties! While opposed to the death penalty, were they still alive, I'd countenance it for the Hill sisters.

(I have neither time nor the energy to go through the legal arguments about the effing song but, to be on the safe side, if you must sing it, please do so in private as public performances might lead to litigation).

Add to the woeful wail of the awful song, there's the ritual of the birthday cake. Fortunately, there was no attempt to provide one for my 85th. Even in cold weather 85 candles would pose a fire risk, whilst during the bushfire season you'd be charged with arson. In winter, it might trigger smoke alarms. And lacking lung power, I'd require a leaf blower to snuff them out.

At my age the ceremonial cake is more like a funeral pyre.

But back to the other dirge. Though a Republican, I've always felt pity for the incumbent monarch who pays a heavy price for being sent happy and glorious, long to reign over us, by the second worst song. No HM can go a hundred yards without being forced to endure yet another rendition, often by a full brass band. Talking of royalties, I hope the royals are paid for this most jingoistic and jangling of jingles, surely entirely destructive of any lingering traces of patriotism. Imagine poor Elizabeth II. How many thousands of God Save My Gracious Me's had she to endure while we abject subjects stood to attention?

Give me la Marseillaise anytime. We've heard it a lot during the Paris Olympics – and every time I was ready to form battalions and storm the Bastille. Whereas Advance Australia Fair, the anthem foisted upon us by Gough, fully justified his Dismissal. It was HM's way of punishing us. Thank you, music critic John Kerr.

Admittedly it's tricky to pen an inspiring anthem when the only words that rhyme with Australia are dahlia, regalia, genitalia and, sadly, failure. But who the hell is this Gert who lives by the beach?

When up for debate in the Whitlam years, the popular choice wasn't Gert but another girl entirely. Name of Matilda. But Gough refused her invitation to waltz and vetoed our unofficial anthem because he felt it would be insufficiently dignified for formal occasions. Like state funerals. Not sufficiently solemn for Gough's sake? When it's a dirge about a suicidal swaggie?

Salesman

Live theatre – that most ancient and odd of the arts. People put on costumes, paint their faces, stand on stages and pretend to be someone else. Mouthing words written by someone else. Written by someone else. Like Ray Lawler or Arthur Miller

Vale Ray. A few weeks ago, Ray Lawler, author of *Summer of the 17th Doll*, died at the age of 103. To my shame I'd presumed he'd been dead for years, even decades. It should have been a day of national, even international mourning as many in the know regard Ray's *The Doll* as one of 20th century theatre's finest works.

After writing over thirty drafts Ray saw his Doll open at the MTC's Union Theatre in 1955, with the author playing Barney, one of the cane-cutting characters. Productions followed in Sydney, London and New York. There was a best-forgotten US film with Ernest 'Marty' Borgnine, Angela Lansbury and Anne Baxter – and an all-black production from the Negro Ensemble Company.

Culturally cringing? I was more impressed with another working-class drama, first performed six years earlier. The Australian premiere was also at the Union Theatre, also by the MTC. It was and remains one of the most important nights of my life. Frank Gatcliff as Will Loman in Arthur Miller's *Death of a Salesman*.

A democratised tragedy – not about Gods or Kings but an ordinary bloke. Willy Loman reminded me of my salesman Uncle Eddie Briggs. A play every bit as relevant to Australia as *The Doll*.

While I never got to interview Ray one of the highlights of my 33 years at the ABC was an hour with Arthur Miller. Who seemed both surprised and pleased I avoided the subject of Marylin. (Although he kept returning to the topic of his famous missus).

First and foremost I wanted to thank Miller for *Death of a Salesman* – and for that memorable night in Melbourne, so far from Manhattan. So Arthur took delight in retelling what happened when the curtain fell on his Opening Night in 1949.

Nothing.

'Total silence,' said the playwright. 'Stunned silence – that seemed to go on forever. Then a few tentative claps swelled into thunderous applause.' 'Applause,' I suggested, 'that has never stopped.'

Since the MTC production with Frank Gatcliff I've seen Willy played by as many actors as have tackled such great tragic figures as Prince Hamlet or King Lear – most notably here in Australia by Warren Mitchell and Anthony LaPaglia. Other Willies? Dustin Hoffman, Brian Dennehy, Lee J. Cobb, Philip Seymour Hoffman, Frederick Marsh – and scores more from the players' pantheon.

'Honour must be paid to men like this,' says Loman's grieving widow' at his graveside in the final moments of Miller's masterpiece. This must be dramas' most memorable graveside scene since Hamlet came across poor Yorick's skill.

'Honour must be paid.' Not just to kings, let alone to gods. But in the age of democratise drama to ordinary people like Arthur Miller's salesmen and, yes, Ray Lawler's cane-cutters and their girlfriends of the 17th kewpie dolls. And most certainly to the likes of their creators.

Arthur Miller (1915-2000) and Ray Lawler (1921 to 2024).

(Footnote. As a young actor Barry Humphries was a member of the MTC, and told how Edna Everage was crested to amuse fellow actor while touring rural Victoria in a bus. The play was Shakespeare's *Twelfth Night*. It's director? Ray Lawler. Such is the magic of theatre).

Billions

As of 6.45 this Saturday morning the total population of our planet was 9 billion plus or minus a few recent arrivals since breakfast. That's out of 100 billion who've lived since Eden or human evolution, given your religious or theological views. Yep, quite a few of us, despite family planning, the pill, the condom and the overturning of Roe versus Wade by the US Supreme Court.

When talking about population I'm being bigoted. This is the HUMAN population – not the total number of rabbits or microbes, the latter being somewhat more numerous. Humans only really count humans, which seems somewhat egocentric. But as we organise any census, we get the say.

And our type of 9 billion figures started only around 60,000 -100,000 years ago. So, when it comes to breeding the fecund bunny comes a poor second. And our number has gone up steadily despite hiccups like wars, famines and plagues – from the Black Death to Covid.

For this, we can blame, if you'll excuse a three-letter word, sex. That's not particularly the Original Sin. Don't blame yourself. God or Evolution shouldn't have made it so pleasurable, second only to eating.

And to make matters worse many are living longer than nature, or the Bible intended. We were allotted three-score-years-plus-ten by God and some miscreants are lingering longer. ('Guilty m'lord' confessed this octogenarian). A few will kick on until they get an official tweet from King William at Buck Palace.

This brings us to the importance of Guinness-type Records. It is a statistical inevitability that someone has to be the world's oldest, tallest, fattest, richest and most obnoxious. Currently, the world's richest person is, like so many billionaires, morally bankrupt. Sadly, this worthless man is worth (?) $300 billion – and his bestie will be the world's most obnoxious individual who's worth a measly $7 billion tops. I refrain from naming them for fear of a defamation action.

The world's oldest person – another statistical inevitability – probably the French woman, Jeanne Calmnet, who fell off the perch at 122. The world's tallest? Robert Wardlow from Illinois died in his early twenties at the height of eight-foot-eleven in the old money. The fattest? Fellow American John Brower Minnoch broke the record and the scales by topping 100 stone. That's 635 kilos in the new. He married twice, had two kids, owned a taxi company and worked briefly as a driver. His huge coffin filled two graves to bursting.

As the creator of DENSA, the MENSA for dills, I'm interested in IQ ratings. Guesstimates abound of the most intelligent humans – the likes of Michelangelo, Da Vinci, Einstein, Faraday, Shakespeare and Newton. Surprisingly neither Elon Musk nor Donald Trump appear on the list. Donald reckons he was robbed.

Sadly, this latter category is rendered redundant as human intelligence, so slowly evolving is irrelevant. As of 6.30 am, AI has taken over. MENSA announced its surrender although AI may keep some members as pets. As part of its inevitable triumph, AI will also take over the entire fortune of Elon Musk and become the next President of the United States. Plus the Extreme (oops, Supreme) Court, the FED, the High Court of Australia and the Secretary-General of the United Nations.

All elections everywhere will be cancelled forever. All problems solved. The world population is expected to collapse. Watch this space.

Silence

Sorry, but if ever a songwriter deserved the Nobel Prize for Literature it wasn't Bob Dylan. The most poetic lyricist in musical history isn't Bob or Cole or Ira but Paul. No, not McCartney. Simon.

My very first essay for this masthead, almost 60 years ago, was about a Simon lyric for 'America' – as much a cinematic experience as a song. About being 'on the New Jersey Turnpike going to look for America', a duet with the angel-voiced Garfunkel.

The best of them was/is Simon's hymn to another friend, Darkness, and with it, Silence. Which is what today's column is really about. The increasingly rare sounds of… Silence. Please listen carefully, as this column is in a whisper – as compared to the bullying bellowing of many distinguished and deafening colleagues.

Silence is golden, far rarer than that precious metal. Bring back Marceau and Chaplin. Though deaf for decades I've rarely heard utter, total, restful silence. Silence in which to think. Or not to. In a world of endless noise and relentless racket, humans seem afraid of it. Yes, they might wear noise-cancelling headphones or earplugs, but only to hear recorded music more clearly.

Remember the arrival of the Sony Walkman? In its time as revolutionary as the iPhone. As pedestrians, we were dangerously deaf to traffic, lost in a world not of our own but perhaps going to Scarborough Fair with Art and Paul. Or paradoxically listening to them extolling the sacredness of silence.

The world I grew up in seemed a quieter, calmer place – until Bill Haley shattered the silence in 1956 with *Rock Around the Clock*. And popular music has been getting ever louder ever since – with concerts engaged in a sort of decibel arms race, harming the hearing of generations.

My deafness? Caused by a lifetime of overloaded studio headphones – a clear case for workers' comp. For the rest of you? Turning up the volume of your loudspeakers and turning your cars into motorised boom boxes.

This brings us to the hearing aid – the classic case of a cure being worse than the disease. Plugged into the lugs these uncomfortable appliances amplify everything. Even the highest-tech versions of the ear trumpet increase noise of all sorts – the white, the background, the unwanted. No known device separates the unwanted audio chaff from the needed wheat.

There is, let it be said, life after deaf – and aids do aid. Yet there are times when silence beckons, and you tug the damn things out and cut yourself off from all the racket. Even the conversation of those close to you. 'Sorry, I'm not wearing my aids' becomes an excuse as well as an apology. You can even turn telly into an endless silent movie, relying on subtitles. Even better – most ads don't have them.

For many it's good to be in the Cochlear era – when an implanted device means you can hear the welcome twitter of distant birdies or the worms burrowing beneath you. Even taking comfort in the Twitter or meaningless conversation. But it's also good to be able to sleep through a thunderstorm. Happily snoring in response.

Meanwhile, I've had to abandon a career in radio where deafness is seen as somewhat negative. And the ABC turned deaf ears to my suggestion of mimed interviews. You could hear the silence in the room.

Country Life

I'm tapping out my weekly words at Elmswood, the 10,000-acre property (and we in the bush still prefer that mode of measurement to new-fangled hectares) that's been our home for the past 40 years. The homestead predated our arrival by a century – and the farm produce, among other things, beef, lamb, some wool, honey, olives, olive oil, soap and Patrice's beloved garlic. All 100% organic.

Keep going upstream and you pass Belltrees, the historic home of the White dynasty (including Patrick). Then comes the Packer fiefdom, Ellerston, owned these days by Gret and last-resting-place of father Kerry. Then comes the majestic Barrington Tops National Park.

Three clicks to our left? Our tiny blink-and-you'll-miss-it hometown of Gundy, population around 200. One pub, one church, a cemetery and the little Gundy Store. Head on another 17 kilometres, after driving between famous studs, you arrive at Scone, proudly proclaiming itself as 'the horse capital of Australia'.

There's a life-size statue of a mare and foal – and the names of famous racehorses on plaques embedded in the footpath. Like those of movie stars in Hollywood.

Growing or dying? I remember a picture-perfect train station with a station-master who proudly tended flower beds. For decades it's been un-manned – trembling to the endless coal trains that thunder to and fro from the vast coal mines of the Hunter Valley. Catching the occasional passenger train to Sydney – 300 kilometres away – is now a lonely business.

Surprise surprise. Retailing is dominated by, yes, the duopoly of Coles and Woollies and we've our share of empty shops in the main drag,

Kelly Street, as a consequence. Little hope of them being leased again. The Scone Cinema has been shuttered for decades. Like a set from *The Last Picture Show*, Our long-term bank closed its doors – and its ATM – ages ago. Its building has replaced – by yet another Real Estate Agency. Seems you can't have too many of them. Every Saturday morning I drive to the Scone Newsagency to pick up actual old-fashioned printed-on-paper newspapers, also collecting the weekly orders for a couple of the neighbours. This remarkable large premises is effectively our town's centre. But I suspect its main business is selling lottery tickets.

Almost forgot. Three cheers for the Municipal Libraries of Australia of which we have a decent example. And another three for the small, valiant Scone Memorial Hospital that I've got to know all too well following my most recent health-scare, involving being mauled by a dog.

Dying? Growing? Coming? Going? One of the few hopeful signs for the district- business seems to be booming in the hossie's Maternity. At the local supermarkets it seems prams and pushers outnumber trollies.

From atop Black Mountain in the middle of the farm you can see smoke rising from the power stations Neville Wran had built besides the coal mines.

Peta Dutton (as I like to call him) promised to replace them with a you-beaut nuclear power plant. You can imagine our delight and excitement! Then, sadly, we had a couple of earthquakes in rapid succession. Back to the drawing board.

We await the LNP's Plan B. Meanwhile Elmswood keeps adding to its population of solar panels.

Other news? Having retired from the ABC (after 33 years of a weekly 600 km commute) I am now a full-time farm labourer – and it's time to muster our Shropshire sheep. Lots of spring lambs.

See yers later.

News

Having been in the news business since the age of 12, I fear the end of the paper newspaper. Though I am an online subscriber to quite a few, I prefer the traditional chip-wrapper versions.

Most mornings, I dragged my billy cart through the silent streets of East Melbourne on my daily paper round, tossing copies of *The Sun* and/or *The Age* into front gardens or in the general direction of front doors. After school, I was a street-corner paperboy jumping on and off moving trams.

Two years later, I graduated to writing columns for *The Guardian* – using the pseudonym of Avoca (can't remember why). They were hot Cold War reds-under-the-bed days. No, not THAT *Guardian*. *The Communist Guardian*, published in a back street of Melbourne. A score of more respectable mastheads would follow until, in my octogenarian dotage, I linger on the back page of *The Weekend Magazine*, left to offer my looney left opinions in both paper and online editions.

Newspapers were called fish-wraps because they were recycled to wrap the fish 'n chips of loving memory. They also served as liners for kitchen drawers and the bottom of budgie cages. Speaking of bottoms. Newspapers served as cheap dunny paper. Torn into smallish pieces, bound with pieces of string and hung from nails in proletarian dunnies. Try that with your electronic subscription. (Presumably, this traditional form of recycling was recycled during the Toilet Paper Wars of Covid).

We're told that the era of the newspaper is ending. But where and when did it begin? The Ancients didn't have them. No 'The Roman' or 'The Weekend Roman'. Ditto the Ancient Gyppos or Greeks. (Unless you include clay tablets. Imagine being a paperboy dragging them around in your billycart. Trying to lob clay tablets onto front lawns. Or lug them on or off Melbourne trams).

That early form of social media, the Town Crier, was arguably a vocal and very local version. But it seems the newspaper was born in my beloved Venice. It was handwritten and widely read in the city from 1565. It was jammed with news about Venetian and Italian politics, wars, and stuff like that.

Printed papers? First seen, as weeklies, in Germany from 1605. Arriving in France they were heavily censored – 'freedom of the press' is a more recent notion. From London to Boston, business boomed, but it took the invention of the high-speed printing press to make mass production and mass reading possible. From weeklies, it became standard to write and print dailies.

In London, *The Times* showed it was possible to print – at speed – on both sides of the page. Enter the era of the penny paper – a sixth the price – pioneered by *The Boston Transcript* from 1830. The telegraph was speeding things up by the late 1840s, as would the invention of cheap wood-pulp paper. Behold the modern masthead, made feasible not only by changing technology but also by rapidly rising levels of literacy.

Thanks to social media and addiction to the iPhone, I suspect what we call literacy is now declining – into the language of abbreviation and the hieroglyphs of emoji. And the news itself no longer seems addictive – certainly less popular with the young. Who now gets their news, if that's what you call it, from elsewhere?

And I head for the exit. Dragging my billy cart.

Ambassador Adams

By the time you read this column I will have taken up residence at the new Australian Embassy in Trump Towers and presented my credentials to the new – i.e. recycled – President of the United States (drum roll) Donald J. Trump.

I needed a job. Badly. Having been forced to retire from the ABC on grounds of 'early onset' it's been thin pickings. As you known I missed out on Yarralumla for being insufficiently woke – and was passed over as head of the Reserve Bank despite being eminently disqualified. Given my ignorance of economics.

Both jobs went to women. Need I say more?

Oh, and although Virginia Bell (one of my predecessors presenting *Late Night*) got appointed to the High Court I was deemed too dilapidated and old. This in contrast the US Supreme Court where octogenarians are seen as being in their prime. Just another example where the US is streets ahead.

Then the job of Australia's Ambassador came up. I was sad for Rudd – we're old friends – but he'd blotted his copybook with Washington. Said rude things about POTUS. Call it karma or kismet but Kev got kicked out.

I was deemed acceptable by the new (i.e. renewed) administration because they mistook my award as Republican of the Year (please check my Wikipedia entry) as signifying support for the Republican Party. All Canberra had to do was move our embassy from DC to Fifth Avenue and I was in like Flynn.

I have of course been intensely briefed and taught to speak with an American accent. Correction, accents. But have been drowning in US cinema and telly all my life this was a doddle. You'd swear I was a New Yorker in NYC or a Floridian. Mar-a-Lago here I come.

Time to thank Joe Hockey for the golf lessons. Having only played a round of mini-golf some decades ago I needed a crash course on as full-size course. Having often played with the President, he showed me how to diplomatically lose on every hole. Onya Joe.

It's also time to thank Trumpette Gina Rinehart for lessons in presidential etiquette. (Onya Gina). And goodonyer Scott Morrison – who's long been close to Donald Trump. ScoMo found time in his busy schedule to fill me in on delicate subjects as Pentecostal religiosity and climate change denialism.

I'm going to be a very busy boy. There's ASUKUS – all those nuclear subs to negotiate. Not to mention US bases, Pine Gap and other means of sacrificing our sovereignty in the cause of better US relations.

I'd like to congratulate the Labor Government for their bold decision to hand over all foreign policy to our powerful friends. This may force some redundancies in Defence but will lead to greater efficiencies in our forthcoming war with China

As you may know, I've been a member of AUSFLAG , an organisation devoted to the cause of getting the Union Jack off our flag. It's stuck in the corner like an effing postage stamp – so as to send patriotic thoughts back to Buck Palace. I will now be able to achieve this by having that pommyfication replaced with the Stars 'n Stripes – as we make the inevitable move to become the US's 51st state. It's a foregone conclusion. A mere formality. Top of my list.

The quid pro quo? We get to vote in US elections – for the mid-terms.

And for President Trump's third.

Public Speaking

Sometime somewhere someone opined that the greatest dread for most of us was the prospect of public speaking… of having to make a speech before a live audience. Not even the threat of death came close. The feelings of vulnerability, the fear of making a fool of yourself.

Though President Donald Trump seems immune to that idea, perfectly happy to make a fool of himself at any and every opportunity we can well imagine his predecessor Abraham Lincoln getting the wind up before the Gettysburg Address. Hence his decision to make it short? Duration? Two minutes. Word Count? 272. No microphone, no autocue, no recording devices. Yet it still resonates. We still heard it loud and clear – from that 16th presidency to Trump's 47th.

(Of course the Address is chiselled into the Lincoln Memorial – soon to be flanked by an even larger sculpture of Trump – second only to the Donald's huge head currently being added to Mt. Rushmore)

Public speaking. Did Mark Antony get stage fright before his oration over the blood-stained corpse of Julius Caesar? Was Gough almost lost for words when he spoke over his own political corpse on the steps of Old Parliament House? ('Et tu brutal Kerr? Then Caesar – Whitlam falls').

Clearly not. Like Mark Antony our EGW rose to the occasion.

Paul Keating told me was a tad nervous before his Redfern Speech, arguably the most momentous in Australian history. But this is understandable. A recently discovered and translated scroll suggests Jesus felt trepidation prior to his Sermon on the Mount. And even the greatest performers can 'dry'. Ask Lord Olivier who has felt as frozen in the spotlight as kangaroo in the headlights or when being hunted by night shooter. Another sort of spotlight.

An occasional interviewee – trapped in in the spotlight of my wireless program – was the loquacious Gore Vidal. He too confessed to times when rather than his erudite ad-libbing or referring to sketchy notes he relied on a printed text. He'd begin thus: 'I shall be reading my speech this evening – but will glance up from time to time to create the illusion of spontaneity.'

Politicians have speechwriters just as Mark Antony had Shakespeare. Aided and abetted by words scrolling unseen on the little screens inches from the clustered microphones. Some pollies have prompts – getting cues from the electric wings via earpieces. Few have the chutzpah or the skills to improvise. Keating did of course – he wasn't totally reliant on Don Watson. Nor did Gough need his vocal and verbal doppelganger Graham 'Freudy' Freudenberg.

I once interviewed Mikhail Gorbachev for an entire hour – only to discover his inseparable translator Pavel Pavlevich would answer my question before Gorbachev could. Gorby agreed we could leave Pavel to conduct our entire interview solo.

For those who dread addressing audiences, technological help is well on the way. Not only will AI write your speech, echoing and amplifying your own known views, but it will replicate your own known voice. I recently heard AI's echo of the late Michael Parkinson – with whom I'd had a number of amiable encounters. The resurrected voicer even fooled Parkie's family.

Soon AI will give us the whole human – as hinted at decades ago with the hologram.

So relax. Sit in the audience and enjoy… yourself.

Towers

Though missing out on the Biblical Babel' I've managed to visit Eiffel's Tower, Trump's, Pisa's, London's and the desolating site of the Twin Towers.

But today I'm taking you to visit my favourite towers, seventeen comparatively spindly efforts (the tallest is 100ft) in Watts, a somewhat bleak suburb of Los Angeles.

Largely a ghetto for African Americans, Watts is famous – notorious – for the riots of 1965. Incited by the racism of the LAPD the riots – also known as the Watts Rebellion – led to 34 deaths, 1,032 injuries and 3,438 arrests. Plus $50,000,000 in property damages. 14,000 National Guards were called in tlo quell it. LA would not see anything on this scale until the LAPD's brutal beating of Rodney King.

Fortunately, the Watts Towers survived the fires – only to face destruction by civic authorities.

Built by one man from scrap – Italian immigrant Sobato (aka Simon) Rodia – over 33 years between 1921 and 1934. 'Sam' as locals called him. Using scrap rebar and decorating his tower and their surrounds with mosaics made from 'found materials' – soft drink bottles, crockery, cracked mirrors and shards of tiles, mostly brought to him by local kids. The final effect reminded me of the paintings of Klimt.

Rodia's small on-site cottage was destroyed by fire on Fourth of July 1956. Not long after Sam had a mild stroke and fell from one of his towers. Tired of fighting local authorities for permits – and saddened by some locals vandalising his efforts – Sam simply walked away. He gave the property to neighbours, to live with relatives, dying eleven years later in 1965.

Never to know that his Towers would gain international fame – and be given the national heritage recognition and protection they deserved.

The site was bought for just $2,000 by two locals from the movie business – and they continued to fight the same local authorities. By now officialdom was intent on pulling the Towers down, deeming both unsightly and 'unsafe'. But a growing protest group – with world-wide support – conducted engineering tests that proved the Sam's Towers were – as it's said – 'strong as steel'.

Feelings then changed dramatically. After years of private guardianship Los Angeles made up for its hostility and neglect by paying for restoration – rust issues and damage to the mosaics plus slight damage from an earthquake. Finally the Towers gained official protection. It's now a National Landmark.

When I first visited in the early 1970s the district was still tense, locals suspicious and even hostile to white faces. Given Watts' bitter history that was hardly surprising. So it wasn't easy to persuade a cabbie to make the trip. But it was worth it. The place, this giant work of sculpture, is magical. And the details of the mosaics are enchanting.

(You can still see the brand-names on Sam's broken soft-drink bottles. The place, among other things, is a monument to recycling).

So next time you're in LA, add Watts to your agenda – as well as Rodeo Drive, the stars in the pavement, Beverly Hills and, yes, Disneyland. See the masterpiece of Simon Rodia. He's as big a star as any in Hollywood.

PS. Don't forget to visit the architectural dream of another eccentric immigrant – also using recycled materials: Justus Jorgensen's magical kingdom – the Montsalvat Artists' Colony on a hill at Eltham. Also deserving of recognition and protection. Part of my life since childhood.

Cops

Repressed memories? If only. In my experience the memories you'd like to repress are the ones that remain most vivid, not so much diminished as intensified by the passing of tine.

It's over fifty years ago and I'm driving down the middle of St Kilda Road towards the Junction. Driving slowly, as its raining. Passing a parked ambulance I see the crew's faces illuminated by the dashboard lights. I distinctly remember thinking 'you won't get me'. Seconds later a human body comes smashing through the windscreen and is wedged halfway into the car. The ambos are there instantly, as I stagger into the roadway. The bloke had stepped off the island and the fish 'n chips he'd been eating were scattered across the road. And there were his false teeth.

Off duty the ambo came to the police station to sign witness statements. 'It wasn't the driver's fault'. Later blood tests showed the bloke had been drunk. But the most powerful memory within those memories? The kindly cop being consoling – and making me a cup of tea.

And now I find myself writing a tribute to the police as first responders and as the heroes they so often are. Think of the policewoman at the Bondi massacre.

Decades later I make a cup of tea for a cop. I'm living in a 120-year-old house in Darlinghurst, deeply asleep on the third floor, when a young officer shines a light in my face. A burglar alarm has malfunctioned and sent a signal to the legendary, even notorious, Kings Cross Police Station a few blocks way. He's had to scale a high security fence to get inside. 'Ripped me uniform' he says.

In gratitude and embarrassment I put the kettle on. It's his first day back after stress leave. An appalling story about cutting the rope and taking down the man who'd hanged himself, defecating in the process. The constable had needed psychiatric help but little was available. 'There are only two shrinks to help all of us in NSW".

Things are better now. In response to the fact that so many cops left the force within a few years. The traumas of the first responders – to accidents, murders, suicides, violent attacks. Policing, like soldiering, is a profession that mass-produces PTSD.

We sat together and talked for hours, before he limped off to have a scratched leg looked at and his uniform repaired. Thanks Mr Plod.

Living in the bush we've had many reasons to admire the local cops. They're helped with cattle rustling, with a robbery, a home invasion, with fatal accidents on Gundy Road. They even donned protective clothing to keep an eye on us when we were quarantined with Covid. Uncomplaining, efficient, decent.

Yet so used to being hated. And I confess to being bitter when caught by the Highway Patrol in speed traps. We know the body count of our soldiers in wars from Gallipoli to Vietnam but I've no idea how many cops have died in the line of duty. But the dead are many. As are the numbers mentally maimed. And they don't have monuments.

It's a dark and dangerous life. And those who volunteer to take part deserve our respect, our gratitude and understanding. Bad apples? Bad decisions? Of course. But so many wholly admirable human beings. I'll put the kettle on.

Pud

Religions of all sorts have traditional food and drink for special occasions. Think the eucharistic mysteries of the wine and wafers at Mass. Think multi-level wedding cakes and Easter eggs. In Greek Orthodoxy Baclava is made with 33 layers of dough – referring to the years of Christ's earthly life. Think ANZAC biscuits for that most sacred of occasions, ANZAC Day.

But for your ancient scribe this is the time to think of the (drum roll) Christmas Pudding, aka the Plum Pud.

I was raised by grandparents on a tiny farm where our fare was simple. Working-class tucker. Corned beef and spuds with the occasional rubber chook freshly decapitated by Grandpa – bringing to life (or death) the term 'rushing around like a headless chook'. To be fair Nanna was a crook cook but she had one piece-d' resistance. Drum roll. The annual Christmas Pudding!!

Following a family recipe handed down from generation to generation, going back to the birth of Christ, it was made of mysterious ingredients and dangled from strings over the kitchen door. Shrouded in a pudding cloth – also handed down from generation to generation – it was the size and weight of a medicine ball... and was the centre-piece of Christmas dinner. With a sprig of artificial holly on top. But it was what was inside that mattered.

No, twas not the look, smell or taste (marvellous though they were) that led to the enchantment of my 5 year-old self. It was the hope of striking gold – or at least silver – within that steaming globe. For concealed beneath the pud's leathery hide there were 'threpenny bits' – threepences that Nanna had collected for the seasonal purpose and boiled to sterilise. Plus a few sixpences. Thrust into the flesh at the end of a knife blade.

(In this cashless society small change is no more. And it cannot be substituted by Bitcoin or credit card. Presumably similar problems are experienced by ex-diggers wanting to play two-up on ANZAC Day)

Ah the joys of Christmas Dinner! Hoping your slice of pub contained some precious coins! And the thrill of seeing the glint of metal! Or hearing its clink. I now know that Nanny cooked the books as well as the pud and made sure her grandchild struck it rich.

Similar discoveries were being made all over Melbourne – as was evidenced by the traces of pud that could be seen when buying tickets from the tram-conductors – until about the end of January. By when the last traces of pud had finally worn off.

Pre-cooked Chrissy puds started appearing in the supermarkets months ago. Not mummified in pudding cloths these days but in plastic tubs ready to heat and eat. And, even more sadly, tragically they contain no coinage. To prevent sparking and arcing in the new-fangled microwave.

What a waste of promotional opportunities! We could have Pud Wars between Coles and Woollies – each claiming to proffer more 'cash back'. To help with cost-of- living pressures and good PR for the duopoly with its fake discounts. There must be thousands of tonnes of unwanted pre-and-post decimal coins waiting for semi-religious recycling. But it's probably just used for landfill.

What price tradition? The Royal Mint could make a mint minting special sterilised threepences for Christmas puds. Plus special pennies just for ANZAC Day two-up games. Take note Jim Chalmers and the Reserve Bank.

Happy Christmas. And Happy Pud.